A collection of "God Moments"

Did You Fill Your Tank?

By Karen Kuluz Hubbard

Authored by Karen Kuluz Hubbard

Cover design and Editing by Davina Rush

About the Author page by Amy Okeefe

Prepared by Inky Owl Publishing

ISBN-13: **978-0692348307**

ISBN-10: **0692348301**

I dedicate this book to my God—
Without whom, I am nothing.

Content

Foreword
A note from the editor

I was so blessed to meet Karen about 2 years ago, around Christmas time (you can read about our meeting in the story of *Giving*, on page 82). When we first met, I was in need of something in my life and I didn't even *know* what it was. I didn't fully understand the powers that were at work until much later— little by little throughout our friendship, but even more so when I sat down to read over the manuscript for *this* book.

As you'll read in the story of Giving, Karen came to me a couple of years ago with the Holy Spirit guiding her firmly in my direction. He had plans for these two women— each of us with a part to play. In our first conversations, we found that we had a common interest in writing, as she told me about this collection of God-inspired letters that she had written to friends. She told me how she would love to have them printed and bound as a gift of inspiring "God-Moments" for her friends.

More and more, over the span of our friendship, I wanted to help her to accomplish this dream. She had already done so much for me personally, and I had witnessed her work with others— she is such an inspiration! I have watched her baking food to take to sick friends, getting together donations to deliver to those in need, on the phone coaching people with her ever-positive channeling of the message, lifting the downtrodden souls around her to stand again in glowing radiance. This woman is on a mission!

"What *is* her mission?" you might be asking. In my view, her mission is quite simply to be a true vessel of God— to show everyone that they are loved, eternally connected to god and *never* forgotten. I feel this, because it wasn't that long ago when I myself had felt forgotten— a broken young woman, just trying to get by with her two kids, when this angel of mercy reached out to me, picked me up, dusted me off and told me, "You were *not* forgotten, *God loves you.*"

That always seems to be the underlying spirit of her message— you are NOT forgotten and you are LOVED, you are a child of God!

So, when it finally did come time to work on this project, I sat down thinking how very glad I was to finally be doing something really worthwhile for this amazing woman who had blessed my family in so many ways. But, I soon realized *again*, that it was *her* helping *me*. God does work in mysterious ways!

As I sat down to look over her words, I was surprised. Page by page, message by message, I was inspired. I had gone through some stressful times in my life and still harbored a lot that I didn't even realize. It wasn't until I sat down, reading over these letters, that I realized how much I needed those *exact* words; "Did you fill your tank?", "The power of words", "put away your dry-erase board", "Love doesn't keep score"— too many to list! I sat there in awe at the timing of these messages— tears in my eyes and smiling at the same time. Again, I was not forgotten. The message had found me and lifted me up at just the moment that I needed it. Just as I hope it will find you, the reader.

I am so honored that Karen has asked me to help her in this project. It has been such a blessing! Thank you Karen, for being the beacon of light that you are in this world!

A collection of "God Moments"

Did You Fill Your Tank?

By Karen Kuluz Hubbard

Did You Fill Your Tank?

When Hurricane Isaac was in the gulf and we were preparing for its possible landfall, I had several people ask me if I had filled my tank. They were meaning, had I filled my car with gas in case the storm hit and fuel was hard to come by. I recall vividly, after Katrina, trying to get to my family on the Mississippi coast and filling my tank for the last time in Gulf Breeze. I remember seeing people stranded in their cars, having been there overnight waiting for the stations to get more gas. There was no more gas from Ocean Springs to Gulf Breeze; all of the stations were empty.

I was at home today, sick and lying in bed, trying to get some rest before the kids got home for early-release. I really don't like those days; there just never seems to be enough time to get stuff done. So, I'm not feeling well, but realize that I have a lot to do in a short amount of time. I was fretting, and God literally told me to *go lay down*. I felt like He gave me *permission* to go get in bed, so I did. As I was lying there, feeling like I should use this time wisely to read something powerful, or watch a sermon, read my Bible, or memorize a scripture, He spoke to me again…. "REST". I wouldn't listen. Instead, I flipped through *The Five Love Languages,* by Gary Chapman— I mean, that is an awesome book and I needed to remember some stuff from it. I briefly glanced at the section, "What happens to love after you get married" (which is a good question), and then flipped over to "Keeping the love tank full", but as soon as I got there, God instructed me to *close it*, and to REST AND LISTEN TO HIM. So I did.

I felt like I was in that space between awake and sleep, thoughts rushing in my head. I had a vision of me going from gas station to gas station, in search of gas, but all the pumps were empty; the nozzles were covered with brown paper bags, like they do when they are out of gas. I backed the car up and around to try another one, and again empty. I thought about what I was seeing and its meaning in my life today…

MY TANK IS EMPTY…..not my gas tank, but my love tank. I go around from place to place, to people, to things, to activities, to conversations, trying to get it filled. Sermons, books, thoughts— But no one has the fuel that I need. No object, or word, no book, no individual has what I am in need of. Sometimes it feels like my husband does. I get an encouraging word, or touch, and I get about a gallon, but how far does a gallon of gas get you? Especially in my big ole SUV? Especially in my needy, baby girl kind of existence? I get some encouraging truth from a friend, a call of concern and I feel loved, but it is fleeting— Squashed out entirely when I feel unappreciated by my children after working hard for their needs and desires. It feels like there is a gaping hole in my fuel tank, with gas running out everywhere. I sure hope someone doesn't light a match, because a raging fire could start! And it has, on several occasions LOL (Outbursts of anger), but It's not really funny.

So, my tank is nearly empty and I go around frantically trying to get it filled. The problem is, I'm going to all the wrong stations. What if we knew there was a gas station in town that we could go to, fill up every day, and it never ran out; it was free of cost, and all we had to do was take the time to sit there, and get our tank filled. We would have no need for all the other gas stations. We could just go to them for candy, or beer and ice, lottery tickets, or a Coke Icee. Just for enjoyment, fun, refreshment.

This morning, God was reminding me that HE IS MY STATION! He has the power, ability and desire to fill me with His NEVERENDING Love, all day long. He wants to, He longs to, He sits and waits for me to come to Him. He is always open, His tanks are always full, and have more power than any love another human being can give me. I cannot love without this filling. I have nothing to offer my husband, my kids, my friends without His love. Why don't I go there every day? I know this, I do. Why do I choose to go my own way and get through my day without His Filling? His presence offers us so much— fullness of Joy, wisdom, answers, peace, rest, and increased faith. Why don't we go there? How do I think that I can even function for one day in my crazy life without it? I can't. I do such a poor job on my own.

I hate the version of me that goes around with an empty tank, asking for people to fill it. I am realizing it is not that people can't or won't, but that what I am looking for, they don't have, and never will. It is like trying to put diesel in my car; it won't run on that! I won't run on love from my husband or acceptance from people, or worldly successes. My purpose in life, the reason I am still here, is to share the love of God with others. How can I share something that I barely have for myself? If my car was running on empty, I doubt I'd be able to lend you any gas.

We gotta get filled up! We gotta STAY ON FULL!! It is a *daily* thing. A daily meeting with Jesus, in His Presence. Sometimes we don't even know that we are lacking, and only He can fill the places that HE KNOWS are empty.

"And I pray that you, being rooted and established in love, may have POWER, together with all the Lord's holy people, to grasp how wide and long, high and deep is the love of Christ, and to KNOW THIS LOVE that surpasses knowledge- that you may be FILLED to the measure of all the fullness of God" —**Ephesians 3:17-19**

Get with God today! Let Him FILL YOU UP TO OVERFLOWING!!! Then we can enjoy our husbands, our families and the people in our lives, needing nothing from them because we are full. Now, I'm headed to the gas station to get an Icee!

I love you, Karen

DO SOMETHING

Piper came home yesterday with some disturbing news about one of her classmates. She gets right off the bus saying, "Mom, Caroline's mom died, and her dad's in jail, and now she is living in a shelter". I, of course, asked her where she had heard this, and that it may not be true; but she was convinced of its validity. My heart ached. This is the child that Piper has had a heart for all year. She had come home one day concerned that Caroline always wore the same clothes. Then, other days she would come home mad because Caroline had been mean to her, or was talking bad about her. The next time she was asking to buy Caroline a birthday present, and then a Christmas present. I tried to convince her not to, because how could she explain to her other friends that she was only getting a present for Caroline? But, Piper insisted, saying she was worried that her friend wouldn't get any presents, because she wasn't sure Caroline had parents, since she had never seen them before. This is in prissy little Destin!!!

So, I investigated Piper's story. I emailed her teacher, just to let her know what was being said on the bus. She wouldn't confirm or deny it, but said that the guidance office was handling it. I know there are rules of confidentiality, but whatever. My heart continued to ache. I awoke today at 5am, unable to sleep with Caroline on my mind. Could you imagine one of *your* kids sitting in a shelter after learning you had just died? To be with strangers, in a strange place? It broke my heart. I went to school this morning and talked to the assistant principal, who is a personal friend of mine, as well as a really strong Christian. She confirmed that the information was true; that the mom had been sick for a while and had died, and that Caroline was now at a shelter. Then, sadly and regretfully, she told me that they (the school) had been so busy this week and had not dealt with this. We shared a moment of regret and shame. Yes, I too was ashamed!! I was ashamed to think that there was a classmate of my child's whose mom had been dying right here in Destin, and we didn't even know it. I was ashamed that I had not done anything for this family, ashamed that I was too busy doing stupid things to even care what was going on around me. My own 9 year old daughter had noticed. She had been trying to reach out in the best way that a third-grader could. Why weren't we aware as a community? This school is small, it is a close knit group of people.

I asked Shellie, the assistant principal, to find out what I could do, and then I waited for her to call back. As I was driving home, I asked God to show me what I was to do. I would go get her, let her stay with us until they could arrange her situation— or Piper and I could at least go visit her, or go get her and take her to Fat Daddy's Arcade. That was my plan. Her mother had just died for crying out loud! — Or I could just pray, whatever you say God, I will do it. The only faint thing that I heard was, "DO SOMETHING".

So I called Hayden, to give him the news. He was not surprised to hear me say that I wanted to foster this child, and surprisingly even to me, he was open to the idea. Every plan that I had made for this Friday was suddenly being pushed aside, and I waited in anticipation for Shellie's call of what to do next. It came quickly, and with good news. She couldn't give me much info, but she had learned that Caroline was now with family, and being cared for, probably better than she had been with her parents. She would be moving and not returning to our school. I encouraged Shellie to talk with Piper's class and to at least give them *some* information. Though they are little, their hearts are so big! They care, and they want to help. So, she was going to check with the principal to make sure it was ok to talk with the class and maybe even give them the opportunity to write Caroline a card. So, there was nothing for me to do for Caroline; I won't be a foster mom after all— at least not today!

This whole thing really got me thinking. WHAT AM I FREAKIN DOING??? I am so busy rushing my kids here and there, complaining about my busy life, that my eyes are closed to the lives of the people around me. I mean honestly, when would I have the time

15

to reach out to anyone else? I'm so busy with MY 4 kids. And it is *wrong*. At least for anyone claiming to be a Christ follower, it is wrong! The Word says that we are to be the hands and feet of Jesus; if we see a person in need, and we have a way to meet it, we are supposed to do so!! But, most people are like me, too busy to even SEE any needs; or to stop long enough to look deeper. We assume social services will take care of stuff like that, right? Our world has convinced us that we can be sued for butting into other people's business. And all the while there are children suffering daily: hungry, abused, hurting, lonely and maybe right next door. Someone who knew this info about Caroline beforehand could have brought it to our attention. There are people out there, many who want to help; people that realize, as Christians, we are called to serve the lowliest. I am tired of government red-tape. I am tired of the false notion that our government takes care of things and that I don't have to do anything.

I have recently been watching "Downton Abbey", a series on PBS. It is about a wealthy family and their servants, in the early 1900s. Back then, there were no Social Services. People just helped each other. In one episode, one of the maids gets pregnant out of wedlock. Her superior in the house secretly brings her food; the rich owners of the Abbey are aware of it and ok with it. I mean, she and the baby would die otherwise. People back then just helped each other. They saw a need, and met it if they could. They butted into each other's lives *without fear*!

God, please continue to open my eyes to what YOU want me to see, and tell me what to do. I believe He will direct my steps. Instead of being too busy with my own life to even hear Him, next time I am going to listen and act. Could I have made a difference in Caroline's mom's life? Does she know Jesus? Is she in heaven? Regretfully I don't have an answer and that is sad.

I want to spend my days doing things that matter to God. Doing things that actually make a difference!!! I am tired of wasting my time. I want to DO SOMETHING!! Do you??

First Corinthian LOVE

I know, like me, you have heard this scripture many many times; the "Love" one— the one they always read at weddings— "love is patient, love is kind…" etc. etc. When is the last time that you actually sat with your Bible and let God speak to you through *this* verse? Well, I was at Amy's the other day, and as we sat at the bar in her kitchen, God gave us a LESSON on it. It was like I had never heard the scripture before.

If God is love, then THIS is what He wants to express to His people. He wants this love to come out of those of us who claim to be Christ followers. If we do not have this love and express this love, WE ARE NOTHING. The biggest commandment that Jesus gave, was for us to LOVE God with all our heart, soul, mind and strength; and to love others and love ourselves!

As Amy and I examined this definition of love, we quickly realized that it is impossible to love like this, even a little bit, without God doing it through us. So, just realizing that I am nothing and that I fail continually at it, even when I try, I believe this is the first step— surrender to God and let Him rule my life, so He can love people through me.

So, let's look at this definition. If I want to Love my kids, my husband, my friends and even strangers, THIS is what I must do:

LOVE IS PATIENT: It is not in a hurry, not rushed, not speeding through each task or each conversation. When I hurry, I AM NOT LOVING THE PERSON. Time is in God's hands… there is ALWAYS ENOUGH TIME!!

LOVE IS KIND: Kind thoughts, kind words, acts of kindness… that is *real* love.

17

LOVE DOES NOT ENVY: In your mind, do you envy? Do you have a feeling of discontent or covetousness with regard to another's advantages, success, possessions etc.? Do you look at Facebook and feel this? I know I do at times. When I do, I am not loving that person, or myself.

LOVE DOES NOT BOAST: (to glorify oneself in speech) "Look at all I've done for you", I hear myself boasting to my husband and my kids— I'm not loving them. Or even if I'm just saying it in my head, I am not loving them.

LOVE IS NOT PROUD: Do you know that all arguments involve pride? Have you ever thought, "But I'm right"? God-love is not proud, it is humble.

LOVE IS NOT RUDE: I am convicted on this all the time, now that I read it again— Rude, anything rude I say; the long sigh I make when I don't want to do something, or am frustrated— RUDE!!! I am not loving them! I am not loving myself!

LOVE IS NOT SELF-SEEKING: This, coming from me, "the baby"; I was not taught that the world didn't revolve around me until in my late teens! So, I have a really hard time with this one, but I do realize that I am not loving anyone when I'm only out for myself. We must go against the world altogether to love in this manner.....SELFLESS LOVE!! To Love, expecting NOTHING in return!!

LOVE IS NOT EASILY ANGERED: I'm laughing as I type, because I fail so miserably at this one. James 1:19 is the cure: Everyone should be QUICK TO LISTEN, SLOW TO SPEAK, and SLOW TO GET

ANGRY. Actually listen with God-ears to what the person is saying; it usually is not the words that are actually coming out, but what those words *mean* in their heart— really LISTEN— *that* is loving people!

LOVE KEEPS NO RECORD OF WRONGS: If you can recount what your husband did wrong yesterday, then you have a *scorecard*; you are not loving him. REAL LOVE doesn't keep score. Truly forgive the offense and God CAN erase it from you. Forgiveness is the key to loving His way. "Forgive them Father, for they know not what they do"— If Jesus could say this, then you can too.

LOVE DOES NOT DELIGHT IN EVIL, BUT REJOICES IN THE TRUTH: Makes me think of gossip. That "feeling" we get when we hear some juicy news and want to repeat it. We should delight in HIS TRUTH! Not the truth of the circumstance or what is actually happening in the natural, but what the WORD says on the topic— because that is the TRUTH this is referring to!! There is a Biblical TRUTH for every piece of gossip we come across!! If we can do that, we are loving people.

LOVE ALWAYS PROTECTS: Keeping your word, protecting delicate information, speaking uplifting things about people, encouraging our kids and spouses in who God says they are. Praying over and protecting our loved ones from the plans of the enemy....THAT IS LOVE.

LOVE ALWAYS TRUSTS: If you worry, you are not trusting God. If you doubt, you are not loving. Every biblical promise is TRUE, and it is true for you and your life!! WE CAN TRUST GOD!! Trusting Him is loving Him.

LOVE ALWAYS HOPES: There is no such thing as FALSE HOPE! That is a lie from the pit of hell! If you believe in Jesus, no matter what the circumstance, THERE IS ALWAYS HOPE. He is *my* hope! Keep Hoping!

LOVE ALWAYS PERSERVERES: Love does not quit!! It presses through, it doesn't stop!! You can't love somebody one day and fall out of love with them the next!! REAL LOVE NEVER STOPS!!!

LOVE NEVER FAILS: NEVER!!! IT WILL ALWAYS WIN!! IT WILL ALWAYS COME THOUGH!!! Love is always the right response!!

As I go over this again, I am realizing the misconceptions that I have in my own life about love— about how I love my family, my friends, my kids, my husband. Nowhere in this verse does it say anything about SERVING, or DOING, or WORKING. Yes, it is my job to cook and clean for my family, but if I am not doing each task while exemplifying the above definition of love IN MY HEART, THEN IT IS ALL FOR NOTHING!!!! I am exhausted with all that I *do*, yet all I really want is for them to know that I love them. And ultimately, for them to know that GOD LOVES THEM.

God, write this scripture on my heart, and help me to LOVE the way that Jesus did! Give me first Corinthian Love! I can't do it without you!

God, where did I put the Garlic Salt?

Ok, I've done it again. I went to Target today to get a few things, garlic salt being one of them. And, like always, I was doing 10 things at one time; *multi-tasking,* as it's called. EXAMPLE: putting groceries away, solving a friend's problems on the phone, feeding the dog, changing out a load of laundry— oh, I'll put away that iPod while I'm back here, return to the pantry, try to start dinner. All of this while I'm still on the phone, as if I have nothing else going on, trying to pay attention to what my friend is telling me. So, can you see how (now that I'm trying to prepare dinner) I HAVE NO IDEA WHERE THE GARLIC SALT IS?? You'd think that I would put it in the spice cabinet, ya know, next to say the Oregano, Basil or Pepper. Nope!! It's nowhere to be found in there. I try to retrace my steps. It could easily be in my bathroom— yea, that's where it's needed. Or how about the laundry room— looked there, no garlic salt. Fridge? NO! Kids rooms? NO!! So, what do I do next? Well, of course— DIG THRU THE TRASH!!! Because that's what I want to do during my 4 hours of peace with no kids. NOT IN THE TRASH!!! In fact— I CANNOT FIND IT!!!!

I know for certain that I saw the clerk put it in my bag; she deliberately put it with the food and not the makeup stuff. I KNOW that I got all of my bags, because just last week I had left 4 bottles of Tide at Target, either in my buggy, in the parking lot or on the counter. They never made it home. So, this time at the counter I was reciting my mantra— "Don't forget the bags. Don't forget the bags". So, I am certain that all of my bags made it to the car (And no, the garlic salt is not in the car! Yes, I checked there too).

So, why am I telling you all of this? Because I am OVERLOADED!!! We are ALL overloaded! And just like my friend Kim's computer, I AM ABOUT TO CRASH!!! I'm serious, I am nearing the end— shutting down— blue screen— CRASH!!! I cannot seem to remember ANY-THING!!! My kids will be telling me a story, one where I was present and involved, and I am listening intently, wide eyed with anticipation— because I have no idea how it ends!!! I cannot remember my own life.

So today, I'm talking to God again, while driving, about this issue of mine. I hear clearly a song from my childhood; it was a commercial for one of those country/gospel singers in the 70's (Christy Lane). The song is, "One Day at a Time Sweet Jesus". I hope someone who is reading this remembers those commercials, because I am seeing it in my head like it was yesterday. Anyway— God goes on to say, "ONE THING at a time Karen".

It may not seem like much, but it was profound to me! So, I stopped my car, and really thought about it. ONE THING— just drive; no radio, no cell phone. I tried it and was amazed at how much peace I had. I drove the speed limit, and actually made complete stops at stop signs! I noticed the trees, and the sun— it was a beautiful day! But, it was hard. From my house to Target, which isn't very far, I reached for my phone like 5 times. My mind could not stay focused on just the ONE thing at hand. I had to call the lawyer back, or let me see if I got that email yet— I didn't, but I almost did!

I am now realizing just how OVERLOADED I have become. And this is something "normal" for mothers; we are supposed to be able to multitask and do it all well! Well, I'm *not* doing it well, and I don't think this is the abundant life God has promised me.

The Word says that, *"There is a time for everything."* —Ecclesiastes 3:1 (NIV). There is a time to drive, and a time to text, but they shouldn't be done at the same time! There is a time for laundry, and a time for deep thought and planning for my oldest kids' college choices, but maybe all I was called to do today was the freakin' laundry!

I believe that with all of the iPhones, iPads, i-craps, everything has become so easily accessible; we have learned that we can do just about anything, anywhere, anytime. I mean, in the middle of a court-case recently, where I was the defendant, I was shooting funny pictures of the opposing lawyers to my friends. Maybe I should have been paying better attention instead! One can play Candy Crush while waiting in the line at the post office, or search Facebook and stalk old high school friends while at dinner with one's family. We aren't even *present* when we are *present*!! Are you getting me??

We believe the lie that we are "getting so much done", but at the end of a day all I feel is exhausted, unproductive, and worthless!! How can that be, when I did 100 things for 6 people in this family before 11 am?!

Just because we **CAN** do something, doesn't mean that we should. Maybe I was supposed to talk to that person ahead of me in line at the store, instead of looking at my emails while I was waiting. Maybe I am supposed to actually WATCH THE ENTIRE BASEBALL GAME, instead of texting friends or searching the web for new boots for the fall!

And maybe we aren't supposed to be so accessible, or have so much access to others. I mean, I can text a friend when I know she is at work and we can text-talk; when actually, SHE IS SUPPOSED TO BE WORKING!!! Or, I'm at the Fishing Rodeo, trying to enjoy a night out with my hubby, but I answer at least 5 phone calls or texts— all of them really about nothing urgent. The problem is that if my phone beeps, I feel the need to respond; and I also feel the need to get a response if I ask someone a question by text. What happened to how it used to be, before cell phone accessibility?

Growing up, if we got a call on the house phone between 5 and 7pm, It better be an emergency, because that was dinner time. It was RUDE to call people during those times. But now, anything is allowed. I am guilty of texting people really late at night. I just think, "Oh, they will get it in the morning", but what if I woke them up? That is so rude! Sorry yall! In my defense, the reason I do it is because the thought will leave my brain if I don't ask you or tell you then, so I hurry and get it down on text before it's gone! So sorry. What if I were to just trust that if it is important, GOD will remind me to tell you? I'm gonna try that!

Amy O'Keefe texted me earlier and asked me to Pray. She had just witnessed an accident on Highway 98 where a person on a bike was pinned under an SUV. The first responders had not even arrived and it was traumatic. I felt sick for the driver— that could have been me! I am so busy, so rushed, and so preoccupied when I'm driving, that I could easily hit a biker on the road. It only takes a split second!! THIS WAS A WAKE UP CALL!!!

We gotta stop yall! We gotta slow down! We gotta do ONE thing at a time, and BE PRESENT IN THE MOMENT. We are missing out on life! It is flying by and we are so busy that we are missing it!!

Well, I'm making a change. I'm gonna trust that God will work out HIS PLAN for my life! And everything that needs to get done will get done (Psalm 138:8). I'm going to try to BE PRESENT— in the mundane things of my day and the glorious parts of my day!! I'm going to put down my phone, turn off the ringer and vibrations, and just LIVE!!

So, if you call me and get my Voicemail, don't be discouraged. I'll respond eventually. Instead, let it encourage you to do the same! Quit answering your phone calls or responding to text messages. Be present where you are!

Oh— and I kept searching, but still can't find that garlic salt!!

Love ya, Karen

UPDATE- GARLIC SALT FOUND!!
October 31, about a month later, in my closet, in the stash of Halloween candy. I was hiding it from myself!!

Psalm 112 Prayer for your Significant Other
(Insert name in the blank)

Praise the Lord, How Joyful is _____ who fears the Lord and delights in obeying His commands.

His children will be successful everywhere, an entire generation of Godly people will be blessed.

_____ will be wealthy, and his/her good deeds will last forever.

Light shines in the darkness for _____. _____ is generous, compassionate, and righteous.

Good comes to _____ because he/she lends money generously and conducts his/her business fairly.

_____ will not be overcome by evil.

_____ will long be remembered.

_____ will not fear bad news; He/she confidently trusts in the Lord to care for him/her.

_____ is confident and fearless and can face his/her foes triumphantly.

_____ shares freely and gives generously to those in need.

His good deeds will be remembered forever.

_____ will have influence and honor.

The wicked will see this and be infuriated.

They will grind their teeth in anger, they will slink away, their hopes thwarted.

People of vision see the invisible, hear the inaudible, think the unthinkable, believe the incredible, and do the impossible.

So pray this for _____, and SEE, HEAR, THINK, BELIEVE, and watch GOD DO THE IMPOSSIBLE!!!

FORGIVENESS IS A DOOR

Do you know that Forgiveness is a door? Are you even aware of what not forgiving someone really does to YOU? Or what not forgiving *yourself* does to you? Do you realize what you cannot receive from God because of the un-forgiveness that you hold onto?

I *think* I forgive people, but when I am still mad at my husband, Hayden, for what he said to me yesterday, I have not forgiven. When I'm pissed at my kids this morning because I'm thinking about how they disobeyed last night, I have not forgiven. When someone's name comes up and I get that look on my face, or an uneasy feeling, I HAVE NOT FORGIVEN!

We all know that we are supposed to forgive people. Whether you are a real believer or you know nothing about the Bible, you kind of know forgiveness is the right thing to do. BUT WE DON'T DO IT!!

There are lots of reasons that we don't forgive, and we justify them all in our minds: "Well my husband didn't say he was sorry", or "my kids have no idea they hurt me when they said dinner was yucky", or "oh I don't really care that I wasn't invited by friends having lunch". We don't even realize that forgiveness is needed. Sometimes we don't even acknowledge that we are hurt, so then, forgive what?

FOR EVERY HURT I RECEIVE, I MUST FORGIVE!!
AND DO IT IMMEDIATELY!!

We are constantly being hurt in this world that we live in; and *hurt* people hurt people. When a dog is injured, he will snap at the owner that he usually adores and hurt them, because the dog is hurting. We do the same thing. How many times have I yelled at my kids because I'm pissed at my husband? Too many to count… *hurt* people hurt people. So, realize that you will not be getting through

26

this day without being offended or hurt by someone — that leaves all kinds of opportunities for you to forgive.

When Peter asked Jesus how many times he needed to forgive his brother, Jesus's answer was 70x7... what Jesus meant was EVERY TIME!! He didn't say, "Once he apologizes", or "once you get even", or "only take so much from him and then stop"; no, JESUS SAID FORGIVE OVER AND OVER!!

If you are married or in a relationship with another person, a friend or a coworker, there *will* be hurts— *and* opportunities to forgive every time!

Like I said, FORGIVENESS IS A DOOR— but, a door to what? Well first, Jesus said in Matthew 6, that if we forgive men when they hurt us, our heavenly Father will forgive us. He goes on to say that if we do *not* forgive men when they hurt us, our Father will not forgive us. WHOA! Well, that's enough reason for me to try it. I mess up constantly, so I am banking on the fact that God forgives me. I have to have it! And my part is to forgive others. So, forgiveness is a door to freedom for me from my sins!

What about forgiving yourself? People don't really know all of the sins that I commit. I can hide it pretty good on the outside. But I know, and God *always* knows. And remember, He looks into the heart only, not what we are doing on the outside. So, if we are sinning in our heart with mean thoughts, control, jealousy, rage, bitterness— he sees it all, no matter what we portray to others. God knows EVERYTHING that I have done. No matter who else in this world knows, HE knows and I know. We need to forgive ourselves daily, so we can be set free.

Most people *want* to forgive. Like, if I have a friend who has hurt me, I long for them to come to me and tell me that they are sorry, so I can forgive them and move on. We all want to move past things. But, the apologies rarely come, or months go by, and I just try to tell myself that I'm not really hurt by it. But, if you ask me about that person I may give you a snide comment or a look. I know some of you are laughing, because you know my looks. It's really hard for me to fake things. The thing is, WE DON'T HAVE TO WAIT FOR THE APOLOGY. In fact, it is not even necessary. We can forgive someone genuinely, without ever getting the, "I'm really sorry". We have to!!

When I was going through my divorce, I was really consumed with bitterness and rage; I was cynical and rude— all fruits of my unforgiveness. During that time I was miserable and I got some great advice from my therapist. She said that every time I thought of what Abner or Michael Linn had done to me, or continued to do or say to me, that I was to recite out loud, "I forgive them Father, for they know not what they do". It *really* helped. Every time I had a thought of what they had done to me or my kids, I would say it again and again. I don't really think I meant it at first— I was just trying to do the right thing. But, eventually I began to believe it. And eventually I *really* did forgive them both. Infidelity, the one thing people believe is "unforgiveable"— I was able to forgive.

Now, no bragging on my part because it was all God working in me— I didn't even *want* to forgive them, or believe that they even deserved forgiveness; but, that was irrelevant. The crime, the sin, the offense, whatever happened to you IS IRRELEVANT. I know you may think that is mean or that I'm being insensitive, but it's true. We forgive because it is a command to do so! PERIOD!!

I think believers screw this up worse than nonbelievers. We walk around going to church and preaching this stuff, but we don't *do* it. There are more people offended in Christian circles than in the partying world! You know I'm right people. If forgiveness was really the first priority among believers, there would be unity in the body; Christian families would stay together, the message of Jesus would spread. But, we Christians are too busy holding on to our offenses between each other to even know what we are modeling to the lost world!— This is not the message of Jesus or the Cross!

Well, here I am on my soapbox again, sitting in my towel-wrap, typing this instead of getting ready to go run all of my errands…

I urge you to take a minute and sit quietly. Let the people's faces come before you; those who you know have hurt you in small ways and in BIG, HUGE WAYS. Write down their names, write down the offenses if you have to; and regarding yourself, recall all of the things that you have done that you have not forgiven yourself for, or that you believe God could never forgive. Write them out! And then recite out loud, "I forgive them Father for they know not what they do to me" and, "I forgive myself Father for I did not realize what I was doing to you". Do it every day, because you will get hurt every day— we all do. Jesus says this same thing to His Father all the time about me.

We need the Father's forgiveness. No matter how well you can behave, it is never good enough. All we have to do is confess our sins; He is quick to forgive them and wash us clean, white as snow, pure of all unrighteousness. That is the truth people!!

Ask God to forgive you, and in turn forgive those who have hurt you— and forgive yourself! Forgiveness opens doors!

On Memorial Day I lost my watch

On Memorial Day I lost my watch! I knew it was in the water at the harbor where we were playing. Several people, adults and children, spent time diving down with masks and goggles looking for it, but we left without it— I assumed it was gone. I was sad. It was an expensive watch, a Rolex; but more importantly it had been on my arm every day since Jack had been born. It was a gift for his birth. He is ten. I really would be okay without it, it is just a material thing, but it felt like something had been stolen from me.

The next day I was at a friend's house. I was helping to her clean out her closet and helping her with her clothes and style, while telling her the story. She would not let it go. She felt like we had to find someone who could scuba dive to go look for it. She called her dad, he called his friend and in 30 minutes I was back on the beach showing Charlie and his 16 year old son, Kyle, where we had been in the water. They dove down and began the search. They were down about 20 minutes when they came up to ask again about our position. They had a skiff, which they had dove from, parked out about 15 feet off the beach— I asked if they had looked around it.

As they dove down once again I began to walk the beach and pray. I told God that I knew He could see the watch and if He wanted me to have it I knew I would; but, if for some reason it was time to let it go, I was okay with that too and I really meant it! It wasn't two seconds later that I saw Kyle come out of the water, raising his arm and saying, " I got it!". It had been lying directly beneath where they put their skiff, sitting on the sand in the position it had fallen. Like a satellite locator on ONSTAR, God had them position the boat directly over it!

God is amazing!! He can really do ANYTHING when we release it to Him and really trust in Him to take care of it, no matter the outcome. This was such a God-moment for me. I would never have even pursued finding it if it weren't for Rhonda, whom I probably wouldn't have even talked to that day if I weren't doing something to help her. God's ways are mysterious to man, and we can't figure Him out! But, if we will just talk with Him, and listen to Him, He will guide our steps!!

I don't really care about the watch, but just knowing that my God sees me and hears me, that He guides my steps and answers my prayers— now *that* is the blessing that I will remember every time I look at the time on my arm!

You too can ask Him anything and know that He hears you! The Word says, *"Do not be anxious about anything, but in every situation, by prayer and petition, and thanksgiving, presents your requests to God, and the peace of God which transcends all understanding, will guard your hearts and your minds in Christ Jesus!"* **Philippians 4:6-7**

Love you, Karen

Hey Julie

Hey Julie,

Oh man, I just wanted to write you to tell you how sorry I am that you are going through what you are going through. Like I said, this "limbo hell" is the very worst that it gets. It will not always be like this, you won't always feel this way and it won't always be so rocky!

I do not know many details about your situation and I don't really know you personally all that well; I only know my own experience. And though our lives, up to this point, do have a lot of similarities, our situations are different too. All that being said, I do feel that I must tell you what it is that got me through and truly changed my life for the better.

In short, I was raised in a large, loving Catholic family and attended Catholic Church and school my whole life. But, I did not know God personally and had no need for God. When I went to college, I abandoned any of my former beliefs and just lived for myself. I was a big partyer, smoked lots of pot, did lots of drugs. Thankfully I never really became an addict. I always knew this was just a phase and I was going to get my life together once I finished school— and I did. Quit using drugs I mean, not to say I got my life together. I graduated from college, then nursing school, then I met Abner and got married— assuming I would then live happily ever after. Don't we *all* think that? Then the success came fast! We made a lot of money and accumulated a lot of stuff. We had kids along the way and it appeared, from the outside, that things were going really great. We were successful, growing a business, having a family, traveling— living the American dream.

Throughout all those 11 years I started to question if there really *was* a God and what that life looked like. I really think now, that it was God pursuing me. We all are made with an internal desire to know the God who created us. I think that gets messed up along the way, mostly by religion and how messed up and wrong a lot of it can be. But, I met a friend in nursing school named Kelsey who was a Baptist, a "real Christian", and I wanted what she had. It took me 10 years, but in Sept. 2003 I went on a retreat and actually gave my life to Christ. It was like nothing I had ever experienced before with "religion"— it was about *me and God*. I really felt like a new person. I came back changed, with a new hope, a new way of looking at life. Not that I was now following all the rules— I have never been and will never be a rule follower, but I was different! Little did I know how God was *really* going to rescue me.

I found out in January 2004 that Abner had been having a 2 ½ year affair with the babysitter that I used at the gym. My life as I had known it was all a lie. Praise God that I had found Him just 4 months earlier. If not, I guarantee you that I would have turned back to drugs, pills, men— whatever I could to ease the pain. The pain of it was unbearable!!! I know that you know this pain. But, because I had turned to God, I used Him instead of drugs or alcohol. I read everything that I could get my hands on. I prayed and cried out to Him. I screamed and yelled and was a total mess a lot of the time. Thank goodness I had lots of nannies that raised my kids at that time, because I was completely absent for many months. Just yesterday, I had to find a baby picture for Avery's 8th grade yearbook, and looking through the photo albums I could barely remember any of the events. I was absent.

I had devoted my entire life, for the past 10 years, to Abner and to his dreams— to what he wanted to do with business and growing the restaurants. I had completely lost myself. I was codependent and so so broken. Even before we got married I had these issues, but marriage only made it worse. So, him leaving me, crushed me. What would I do? What was I able to do? I did not believe that I could survive alone. I loved him and wanted our family intact. My parents are still married and I believe in marriage, that it is for-life. I was willing to forgive and stay married. We tried this for over 2 years; we even moved here to try and save it. All the while I got stronger and stronger in my faith and in who God had created me to be. Only God can do that Julie. Only Christ can tell you who *you* really are. He is the Creator! He made me, and had a specific plan for my life!!

So, gradually I found myself and separated from Abner; we divorced in 2006. At the time I still loved him and believed that I would live the rest of my life just loving a man that I could not be with, that didn't want to be with me. But, during that time I got to know God even more. Really, just by spending time with Him. Listening to His still, small voice, or listening to music, or some church service. But it was not religion that brought me to God, or me behaving well. It was a personal relationship that I had sought— and HE CHANGED ME. He taught me who I was and why I was created.

We are *not* what people say we are. In cheating, and the aftermath of all that, Abner said I was worthless, ugly, unattractive, spoiled, money-hungry, snobby, unlovable, stupid, etc etc etc. But all the while, God says I am fearfully and wonderfully made, that I am chosen, that I am His Beloved and that HE has a plan for my life. And, for some reason I just believed Him.

I could feel it working. I could feel myself changing— the way I felt about myself began to change and it was apparent to everyone that knew me. Let me remind you, I was not perfect by any means! I still threw hissy fits and pity parties for myself. I drank too much, escaped by spending too much, I still freaked out, and I messed around with a couple of stupid relationships even; trying to fill that VOID of loneliness.

But all the while, God quietly pursued me and drew me into Himself. Even in the midst of stupid things I could hear Him saying, "No, this man is not your answer". It was hard, but necessary.

Julie, I just wanted to tell you all of this to encourage you!! You are in a horrendous time and full of FEAR. I know it is extremely painful, can feel hopeless, and there are so many hard decisions. I only can speak from my own experience and say, GOD IS YOUR ANSWER!! He can provide EVERY NEED that you are searching for; peace, comfort, security, an everlasting love that has no conditions and JOY that you probably have never experienced before.

No one could have told me 9 years ago, when I learned of Abner's affairs and was so broken, that I could have a life like I do now! I would have never believed it!! And I am not talking about the new husband and family. I am referring to the woman that I am!! The confidence that I have in myself because of the relationship that I have with CHRIST!! It could not have come any other way!! Because this family and life that I have now can also go away. But I am now certain, no matter what happens in my life, I am secure because of who God is to me!! I will survive anything because Christ is with me.

You too can have that SECURITY. You can experience the greatest Love anyone has ever known. You can experience forgiveness, joy, peace, patience, kindness and the goodness of God.

So, look at this experience as your rescue!! He is throwing out a lifeline to a drowning person. Grab hold of Him and let Him rescue you! It is unlike anything you have EVER experienced that claims to be God or religion. I am talking about a personal experience with God. All you have to do is call out to Him and He shows up. He has been waiting for this since the day you were born.

REDEEMED, RESTORED, RECONCILED

On the way to school today Jack told me that his step mom was going on a retreat in Colorado. My first gut-instinct was jealousy. I want to be in an airport, traveling to the Colorado Rockies to be alone with God for 4 days!

After I dropped the kids off, I contemplated what I was feeling. Once I got over the jealousy I knew that God needed me to send her a text.

Let me remind you, this "step mom" is the same young woman that was my former husband's mistress for over 2 years of our marriage. The same woman who came in and out of our lives for 2 *more* years as we tried to reconcile. I have gone through hell with this girl, but also some incredible healing and forgiveness over the past few years.

Well, back to today— So, God prompted me to write her a text. I knew she would be traveling for a while and could receive it before the retreat started tonight. I thought of all the things I could say; "I'll be praying for you", "have fun"— but, when I thought it out, I didn't want her to think I was butting into her business. I didn't want to offend her, or make her worry in some way. Maybe I just won't send one. This is all going on in my mind as I drive home from Lowes.

Now I'm home and God keeps reminding me that I need to text her. I say, "OK, well then you tell me what to say!" All I hear is, "forgiven". Well, if you know the details of my story, most of you know that Michael Linn and I have already crossed the bridge of forgiveness. I have asked her to forgive me on one occasion, and on another I had sincerely told her that I forgave her. It took about 3 years of praying, but one day I just knew that I had sincerely forgiven her and I have felt differently towards her ever since. So why does God need me to tell her again?

Well, as hard as it was, and as much as I wrestled with God about what I thought, I sent a text. It said, "I am praying you hear from Jesus loud and clear about who HE says you are Michael Linn. You are forgiven and free in Jesus' Name. We both are!"

After I finished typing, I was overtaken with emotion. I began to just weep, knowing that it was the Holy Spirit who had penned the text and was working in ME!

I began to recall my own trip to the *Captivating Retreat*— Abner and I had been reconciled, I was believing in complete restoration for my marriage, but I was still SO broken. I went with Gretchen and Jen from Destin, and Gidget and Kelly from Jackson. As I thought about the person I had been that day in the airport, where Michael Linn is today, I sobbed with gratitude over the grace and mercy that God has shown me! How much He has changed and healed me. *That* Karen was broken, doubtful, weak, codependent, consumed with resentment. I didn't even think forgiveness was needed. I was completely justified in hating this girl till the day I died.

God is the great Restorer and Redeemer!! Here I am today writing that same girl a text and sincerely wishing the best for her, as she experiences the same retreat that I attended over 7 years ago. If you would have told the Karen of 2005 that one day I would feel this way about Michael Linn, I would have laughed in your face out of disbelief! But Jesus really can change people. I know, because He has changed me completely!

The *Captivating Retreat* is so dear to my heart. I love what it stands for, about the hearts of women and how God made us. There were many times that I wanted to share what I knew with Michael Linn— I knew she needed it. Although I knew that she couldn't receive it from *me*. But a funny thing happened; I gave the book to a friend in Oxford a few years ago and told her about the bible studies. She ended up starting a study on the book in Oxford and a friend of hers had invited Michael Linn.

God is in charge of everything people!! He can do whatever He wants!! He can use whomever He wants!! When I heard that, I was amazed, but now *this*— HE IS JUST INCREDIBLE!!

As I continued to cry and thank God for all He has done in my life since that retreat, I knew that I needed to share it! Every prayer that I had been praying back then was answered!! Not in the time, or way, that I thought it would be, but they were answered. He is faithful!! No matter what you are struggling with, you can be sure that GOD knows about it and knows how HE is going to work it out when you turn it over to Him.

This is such a picture of redemption. Back then, when I was seeking after God and really trying to know Him and be obedient, He was working in my life. And back then, when Michael Linn was running from God and living her sinful life as an adulteress, God was working in her life too!!! He wanted her too! Our paths were different, but they both led back to The Father!

There is no sin that cannot be forgiven. There is no person that does not deserve your forgiveness. There is no mistake that cannot be made right! Who do you need to forgive or reconcile with? I promise you, in the end, the one who will be REDEEMED and RESTORED is YOU!!!

I love you!

Karen

The Beauty Pageant

Have you ever been to a beauty pageant? Well, I went to the DMS Pageant this week to watch several of my friend's daughters compete. There had been many conversations all week about the controversy of pageants and judging girls on beauty. Man, some people HATE THE IDEA and voiced it *loud and clear*. In fact, one mom had written into the Destin Log complaining about the pageant and saying it should not go on.

Don't get me wrong, I do not support beauty pageants, though I do enjoy watching Toddlers and Tiaras— I met "Honey Boo Boo" and her family at Disney World! LOL I just love Mama June! But, as I listened to people's disgust of the whole thing, it really got me thinking and asking God some questions about BEAUTY.

Are you watching Survivor this season? Well if you aren't it is the battle of the brains, versus beauties, versus brawn. The smart people, the beautiful people and the athletic people. IT IS AWESOME! It's interesting which group is winning so far! You gotta check it out. So, this whole beauty pageant, combined with Survivor, has really got me thinking about how I view all three.

People want to say that the reason they oppose pageants is because of the "judging" of women based solely on their outward appearance; they say this is wrong, AND I TOTALLY AGREE. But what about judging based solely on academic performance, ACT scores, Honor Roll? What about judging based solely on athletic ability or strength? Listen people, our kids are being judged *every* day! We all know people who were born with these gifts, and are judged on it constantly. Some God-given gifts are just more socially acceptable than others in our fallen world. Sadly, I judge based on these things too. It's all around us.

So what does the Word say about BEAUTY? In **Psalms 45:11** it says that, "The King is enthralled by your beauty...." And when Jesus explained the reason that He came to earth in **Isaiah 61:3,** He said, "...to bestow on them a crown of beauty instead of ashes...." In **Genesis 6:2** it says, "...the daughters of humans were BEAUTIFUL...." It also talks of how beautiful Sarah, the wife of Abraham, was. In **Genesis 29** Rebekah was said to be very *beautiful*, and Rachel was lovely in form and *beautiful*.

Females are *beautiful*— every last one of them! God chose to express HIS BEAUTY through the female form when He created her. We *all* possess beauty!!! Beauty comes in many forms, shapes, and sizes. However, what the world thinks of as beauty in 2014 is physically fit, zero body fat, tone, tall, tan, white teeth, straight hair, long eyelashes, smooth skin, big lips, well-formed butt, ripped stomach— but that also changes. Marilyn Monroe would be considered a plus size model these days, but back in her time she was the epitome of worldly beauty. BUT GOD NEVER CHANGES!! And His opinion is that *all* people possess His beauty, because He created us beautiful.

On the other hand, THE ENEMY, HATES BEAUTY. If you read the story, Lucifer was the most beautiful angel before he was cast out of heaven to earth. Therefore, he despises the beauty in God's creation. Why do you think that you feel so attacked when you look in the mirror? Why do you think women are assaulted, raped, prostituted? It is the enemy and His attack on beauty.

I can't help but think that the enemy has skewed every last person's view on beauty, including me. He has skewed what God intended beauty to be. He has skewed the idea that I could be beautiful, and you too.

As I watched the pageant, each and every one of the 29 contestants were beautiful, each in their own way. Each of them had family and friends in the audience who thought they looked beautiful, no matter what the judge's opinions were. I did not even know what they were being judged on. Was it poise, confidence, the dress, how they walked, or their physical beauty, or a combination of all?

There were girls who clearly had competed before, as well as ones you could tell had never stepped foot on a stage. Some were well spoken, and some were jittery. One was poised and another a bit clumsy. But I saw BEAUTY *everywhere*.

God put in each of His daughters the DESIRE to be beautiful! We all want to look our best. If that wasn't true, then we would just wake up, brush our teeth, and head out the door— but we primp— some for longer periods than others. We exercise, get our nails painted, buy pretty clothes, and color our hair!! You who are opposed to the pageant stuff can disagree, but *you* want to be beautiful too!!

Only God knows people's motives for doing pageants. I could only get the experience through my friend's children and *their* reasons for doing it. Their answers were, "It's fun. I want to get pampered. I want to feel like a princess". They wanted to experience this and the fun of getting dressed up with their friends. Not one of the girls that I spoke to were really all that concerned about winning.

I know some of the moms were opposed to this at first. They were concerned about rejection, or the girls getting the wrong idea about beauty. But, after they listened to their daughter's hearts, they allowed them to participate. And they prayed. One mom knew it was God positioning her daughter there. She didn't know the whole reason, but she felt a peace about her doing it. Listen people, WE DO NOT KNOW WHAT GOD IS UP TO. We say that we hate to see them being judged, yet WE JUDGE someone's decision to be in a pageant! We are all messed up.

Well, I know BEAUTY IS IMPORTANT!! That is why it is so opposed. Beauty expresses the heart of God!! He made females beautiful, to express His beauty to the world. ALL people possess

41

beauty!! Some hide it, some are ashamed of it, some have been wounded because of it, some abuse it when they have it, some use it to hurt others and some disregard their own beauty. But, the most beautiful of women are the ones who OWN IT. The ones who know that they have beauty and express it in whatever form. They are comfortable with the beauty they have been given and they express the beauty of God in how they possess it.

There is nothing more beautiful to me than seeing a plus size woman in her bathing suit, confidently walking down the beach. This is way more beautiful to me than my gorgeous friend, with her near perfect figure, lying next to me, that WILL NOT get up to go pee in the water without a cover up on! A woman, comfortable in her own beauty, is GORGEOUS to me, no matter what her size!!

There is nothing wrong with being beautiful, or wanting to be beautiful, or expressing your beauty. I blame the women's lib era for skewing this in women. Since all of that Equal Rights crap, we are told that we are to be strong women, who can do anything a man can do, and that beauty doesn't matter; that we shouldn't just be a pretty face. And I agree!! Women are SOOO much more than just BEAUTY. We are smart, strong and can do many of the jobs that men can do— and better, I might add. But it doesn't mean that we have to give up beauty to have those things! It is not an either/or situation— no matter what the world tells you. No matter how much they stuff it, or ignore it, ALL WOMEN LONG TO BE BEAUTIFUL, because it is the God in us, longing to express Himself!! And ultimately, as **1 peter 3:4** states, "Your beauty is not your outward appearance, but of your inner self, the unfading beauty of a gentle and quiet spirit which is of great worth in God's sight." A beautiful person is one who expresses her beautiful spirit. It is God-given, we each have it.

My desire is for people to own their beauty and to be comfortable in their own skin. It is ok to display beauty. WE DO IT EVERY DAY WHEN WE LEAVE THE HOUSE. NO we are not on stage in a pageant, but I know when I am in my closet getting dressed that I am trying to present my best looking self to the world out there, and that's no different than the pageant stage— some days I try a little harder than others.

I encourage you to walk around today and look for something beautiful in each person that you come into contact with. It's easy really! And in doing so YOU WILL SEE THE HEART OF GOD! He is exquisitely beautiful, and SO ARE YOU!!! SO OWN IT!!

Dreams of a Dreamer like Me

Whitney Houston had a dream. She just wanted to do what was in her heart, and in her soul— SING. She didn't care about the fame and fortune, she actually didn't even like it. She just wanted and needed to get out what was inside of her, through her amazing voice. It was the dream and purpose that God created her for. His beauty reflected through her powerhouse of a voice like no other. It was the only one like it in all of creation and through all spans of time.

Did we get to enjoy her gift for long enough? Did she fulfill her calling and then abandon this earth? Or was her time cut short due to sin and the many ways of the enemy? Or had God seen her suffer enough and rescued her into His loving arms? There is no doubt in my mind that she is sitting at the foot of Jesus right now, doing what is in her heart, singing to her Lord and Savior! I know without a doubt that she knew Him and though she chose to leave him for periods of time in her addictions and fame life style, He was always with her. I know there were moments in her life that she cried out to Him and He answered. But why couldn't she beat it? She had THE POWER in her. Why wasn't that enough? Or did she beat it, through her death?

As I watched the documentary about her life, I saw the innocent, God-Loving young girl being pulled away from her Lord by the things of this world. I listened as her voice, her gift, changed. It was affected by the shift. Did she lose the anointing? *Can* we lose the anointing? Can we squash out the Holy Spirit operating in us? Is it always there once we accept Christ, or can it flee when we go our own way? As I watched her life, I began to fear. Could this happen to me? Has it *already* happened? I know there are times that I get in the world and the worries of the world and forget there is a heavenly call on me.

Whitney's song lyrics say, "I lost touch with my soul, I lost sight of my dreams". Is that what happened? We can easily forget who we are, or WHOSE we are, and be caught up in another life all together. Do I even know my real soul, my prosperous soul? What does that look like? My soul— my mind, will and emotions— I want to have the mind, will and emotions that God has put in me. What are my dreams? Really what are they? What do I most want to accomplish in my life span?

As I hear of other people my age dying suddenly, such as Susan Howorth at age 43 (The speech therapist in New Albany), and Whitney Houston at 46— it makes me realize once again that our days here are numbered. This life is short! Am I even pursuing my dreams or God-given destiny? When do I plan on starting, or even figuring out what my dreams might be? I am too busy doing the rat-race of life to even contemplate it.

The captivating message: we all have a beauty that is all our own to share with the world. We all want to be romanced, we all want to be part of an adventure. What does this have to do with my dreams or purpose?

I'm tired of just living, going through the day to day duties of the wife and mother of 4 kids; house manager, the maid, the cook, the nurse, the teacher, the disciplinarian, the chauffeur, the extracurricular activities coordinator. I want something more. There is MORE in my soul to share in my time on this earth. In doing all of the above duties, when is there time to pursue my dreams?

What is in me that I just need to get out, as Whitney said she *needed* to sing? What is it? To encourage women, counsel them, teach about the princess mentality *and* the everlasting Love of Jesus? I want to get excited about something I am doing, like my husband is excited about coaching baseball. He loves the game, the teaching and growing, he loves the competition.

So what do I dream of doing? Traveling, helping people, encouraging people to live their lives to their full potential, encouraging people to chase their dreams— these are all things that I think about and get excited!

So I encourage you to take a few minutes and allow yourself to dream. Do not think about what you cannot do because it's too late, or because you have too much responsibility, or because you're too old. What dreams did you have as a little girl? If money were no object and you had no responsibilities, what would you be doing? Where would you be living?

Life is short people. Dare to DREAM and see where God can take you!!

CLAIMS

God Calling today was talking about the secret to prosperity; that is, to see God as my only supply of anything and everything that I could ever need and want. It's funny how that is so hard to do. I *say* it's true, I *say* it's what I believe, but I don't actually think or act like I believe He will really take care of all things. If I *really* believed it, I would not have a worry in the world. And, as I type this, I do know in my mind that it's the truth— but I don't really, fully believe it in my heart.

Don't I have a part to play? Don't *I* have to do something to receive the blessings of God? It all boils down to this— will God really take care of me, even when I don't do things right, even when I mess up, when I sin big? And the answer is *still* Yes! At least that is what I would tell someone else. That is what I believe for someone else, but sadly I doubt it for myself. Or maybe I think my wants and desires are silly; they are too much for God to be worrying with. I'm selfish. These are all things that run through my head.

So, *God Calling* goes on to say, "CLAIM ALL FROM MY STOREHOUSE", God's storehouse. Why aren't we claiming what is rightfully ours as Christians?

If I had the winning lottery ticket, wouldn't I go to the state and claim it? If I knew for certain that I purchased it and the numbers matched, I would go stake my claim to the prize. I am the rightful owner!

Webster's defines "claim" as to demand or ask for as rightfully belonging or due to one.

As children of God, as brothers and sisters of Jesus, WE HAVE THE RIGHTS TO ALL THINGS!! I know I do not believe that I deserve the rights to all the good that God has for me. I'm not always the best

Christian, or wife, or mother, or friend. The enemy convinces me that I'm not entitled to those things; they are for the ones who are always in church, serving, talking nice— not for ones like me. I may deserve some things, on some good days, but ALL THINGS? I don't think so.

But the truth is, nothing I ever did has made me worthy of anything good from God. No matter how "Good" I can be by worldly standards, I still deserve death. None of us are good enough. It is by His absolutely amazing grace that I was saved, am saved and will continue to be saved. His mercy on poor, pitiful me is what gives me the right to claim every good and perfect gift that He pours down on this earth! Remember, God sees us as righteous because He sees us through the blood of Jesus. Therefore, He sees us as innocent, white as snow.

So *why* aren't we claiming it? Why aren't the Christians claiming what He has rained down? I think we don't feel worthy— the majority of us don't really know who we are!

I watched Gladiator last night— which is one of the best movies of all time. I love epic movies about the times of kings and kingdoms. Maximus knew who *he* was. He was a man of honor and character; a noble general, a mighty warrior. Even when the others only saw him as a slave, he knew who he was. He eventually claimed his authority and saved Rome by fighting his way out of slavery, as a Gladiator. He knew what belonged to him and he claimed it, no matter what his circumstances were— warrior general or slave gladiator. Before the king died he had given to Maximus the rights of sonship; he called Maximus his son and all authority of the kingdom would be his upon the king's death.

As born-again Christians, we too have that same right! We have been given the rights to claim ALL OF THE INHERITANCE OF GOD!! We are Co-Heirs to the throne with Jesus…..seriously we are!!!

How do you think your life would change if you really walked around BELIEVING that one— believing and claiming all rights to prosperity, health, peace, authority?!! Man, my daily life would look so different. I want to be different. I want to claim *all* He has for me and my family.

I see a room full of lottery tickets, all with winning numbers, just piled on the floor, waiting to be claimed! *Stand up* people! Let God, through His Word, tell you who you are! You are the righteousness of Christ, fearfully and wonderfully made; co-heirs with Christ to the throne, sons and daughters of the MOST High God! The creator of the Universe people!!! That's a pretty large inheritance coming to me!!

CHRISTIANS, let's start acting like it! Not in cockiness or arrogance, but with AUTHORITY, knowing and demanding what belongs to us! Let's see the fullness of God come to pass in ALL areas of our lives; our families, our businesses, our marriages, our relationships, our finances, our NATION!

Over 75 percent of Americans claim to be Christians!! Let's stake our claim in this election, in our government!! We are the majority!!

Seek First My Kingdom

I've been worrying a lot about finances lately. I know I shouldn't, but I have. My mind has been so consumed with thoughts, ideas on how to save, what to do, etc etc. I have a lot of faith for finances, I always have. So this "fear, doubt and worry" has taken me off guard.

As I prayed today, and searched the Word for help, I got to **Matthew 6**, which refers to worry. We all know that we shouldn't worry— it can't add a day to your life, etc etc. But, what I got from *Matthew* was what we SHOULD do: *Seek first the Kingdom of God and His Righteousness and all these things will be given to you as well.*

So, I got to wondering, what exactly is "the Kingdom of God" and how am I supposed to seek it? It doesn't say to "seek God", but rather to seek "His Kingdom". So I began to ask God to show me what this meant.

If I were to live in this "Kingdom" what would it be like? How can I seek to find the "kingdom of God" in the world that I live in, in the country I live in? What laws, principles and customs would that Kingdom have versus the laws, customs and principles of the world that we live in?

Next, God directed me to search my mind for laws and principles that I know are from His Kingdom. Then I went to the gospels and let the Holy Spirit direct me to more—ones that I had previously underlined in my Bible since I have known Christ.

This is what I found:

- ❖ Give when you see a need and you have the means to meet it. Money, time, possessions, comfort, a hug.
- ❖ Forgive ALL things.
- ❖ Do not repay evil with evil, but with good.
- ❖ Treat others the way you want to be treated
- ❖ Guard your heart, for it is the wellspring of life within you
- ❖ A gentle word turns away wrath
- ❖ Do not worry or fret about anything!
- ❖ Act justly
- ❖ Love mercy
- ❖ Walk humbly
- ❖ Be pure in heart
- ❖ Hunger and thirst for righteousness
- ❖ Rejoice and be glad in this day
- ❖ PRAY, ask God for anything
- ❖ BELIEVE He can do ALL things and controls ALL things
- ❖ Turn your cheek to ANY offense
- ❖ Go the extra mile
- ❖ Be honest, tell the truth, it will set you free.
- ❖ PRAY always.
- ❖ Love God with all your heart, soul, mind and strength.
- ❖ Love others.
- ❖ Love yourself, take good care of yourself.
- ❖ If you make a mistake, humble yourself and ask for forgiveness
- ❖ Encourage one another
- ❖ Ask, seek and knock, ask anything of the King, He loves you!
- ❖ Live on every Word from the mouth of God, not on bread alone.
- ❖ Act like the daughter of a King!
- ❖ Rule over the world we have been given.
- ❖ LOVE people!
- ❖ Seek after the people of His kingdom: get to know them, pursue them, and invite them into His love which is in you.
- ❖ Be the salt of the earth!

- ❖ Let your light shine before others that they may glorify Him.
- ❖ Be content in WHATEVER circumstance you are in!
- ❖ Pray for those who persecute you
- ❖ Give to the one who asks you
- ❖ Keep the Faith
- ❖ Settle matters quickly with your adversary
- ❖ Be reconciled to anyone who has something against you
- ❖ Fast in secret, pray in secret
- ❖ Hear Gods Word and put it into practice!
- ❖ Give up everything of this world for the sake of the Kingdom
- ❖ Whatever we bind on earth is bound in heaven and whatever we loose on earth is loosed in heaven. We have been given this key, USE IT!
- ❖ What God has joined together, man cannot separate!
- ❖ Divorce only for abandonment and adultery
- ❖ Husbands LOVE your wives the way Christ loved His church.
- ❖ Wives respect and love your husbands.
- ❖ Do not covet ANYTHING that belongs to someone else.
- ❖ First will be last, and last will be first.
- ❖ Be a SERVANT.
- ❖ Go and make disciples of ALL nations.
- ❖ The Sabbath is for man, not man for the Sabbath. REST FROM ALL WORK 1 day out of 7.
- ❖ Hear the word and the promises and ACCEPT IT!!
- ❖ Whatever you ask in prayer, BELIEVE you have received it and it is yours.
- ❖ Forgive so your father will forgive you.
- ❖ Give and it will be given to you!
- ❖ GO IN PEACE.
- ❖ Run the race, do not sit out!
- ❖ DENY yourself.
- ❖ BE BOLD, ask, seek and knock!
- ❖ Be rich toward God, do not store up things for yourself!

- If you have been given much, much will be required of you, much will be asked.
- Take care of widows, single moms and children.
- God must be greater, I must be less.
- We will not understand what God is doing, we can't. Quit analyzing, and accept this.
- Let your light shine!
- No one who believes in Christ stays in darkness.
- LOVE ONE ANOTHER
- You may ask Jesus for anything in His name and He will do it.
- Love God and obey His teaching.
- Do not let your hearts be troubled.
- Do not be afraid.
- You are clean
- Apart from Christ you can do NOTHING!
- If you remain in Christ and Him in you, ask whatever you wish and it will be given you
- If you obey God's commands you will remain in His love, the one command He states here is LOVE EACH OTHER!
- We did not chose Christ He chose us!
- You will have trouble, whatever it is, He has already overcome it.
- Eternal life: is to know Him, really know the character of God and Jesus
- The Church of Christ will be ONE in Jesus so the world will believe (John17:20) I have given them the Glory that they may be ONE. Brought to COMPLETE UNITY!!
- Let the Love of God and Jesus be in you!
- Seek Peace!
- LOVE ON ANOTHER!

Wow, how different it would be to live in a world with *these* principles, rather than the one I live in every day. So, I feel God telling me to seek out His Kingdom, to seek out these things, and to NOT WORRY!

I encourage you to ask God what seeking his kingdom means to you! I would love to add what you find to my list!

BE ENCOURAGED!

Love, Karen

Weed, Wine, Weight, Worry

Our Bodies are the Temple of the Holy Spirit

Kelly, my dope smoking friend that lives in the islands, asked me to find for her where marijuana is talked about in the Bible. Unfortunately, there is a lot of theological controversy over this topic. There are some who say it was an herb used to make anointing oil **(*Exodus 30:23*)**; but the word that is actually used in this text is *Calamus*, not *Cannabis*. Some modern scholars claim that those who had deciphered the bible for King James translated the Hebrew word wrong. I'm gonna go with the old ones whose translations have survived thousands of years and tons of criticism. Read Exodus for yourself. God was giving Moses the formula for making holy anointing oil, not something to smoke and get high. Kids these days are smoking bath salts too, not saying that's right either.

I do believe that God made all living things, including the Marijuana plant. Hemp has many uses; rope, clothes, fuel, paper, building materials. But, nowhere in the Word of God does it say we should smoke it, or smoke *anything* for that matter. I know that no one wants to hear this, but it's true.

From one former pot-smoker, I really don't enjoy hearing that myself. It was something that I enjoyed doing, but I quit based on the fact that it was illegal and also based on my own conviction by my God. I am not judging anyone else who does it, as I do other things that I know are wrong, we *all* do— but what does God really want to say about all this? I feel that Church and Religion have gotten most of it wrong.

"...Your bodies are the temple of the holy spirit..." **1 Corinthians 6:19**. Do you treat yourself, your body, like you are housing the Holy Spirit? Some churches like to focus on one aspect of defiling the body: Baptists say no drinking, Catholics are OK with drinking but against

premarital sex, Pentecostals think we defile our bodies with makeup, dancing etc., and some think that cutting our hair is wrong.

For myself, I want God to speak to me, through His Word, about what I need to do with MY temple.

Regarding Weed: The Word does not say we can smoke. As we all know, inhaling stuff is bad for our temple. One guy wrote that if God wanted us to smoke, he would have given us a chimney on top of our head. And smoking pot is illegal where I live. So, those are the reasons that I don't.

Wine: The first miracle that Jesus performed involved turning water into wine for a wedding– and it was not a small amount. It was something like 960 gallons of wine! Jesus drank wine. If he did it, then we can do it. Now, *how much* is between you and God. The Bible speaks very clearly that *drunkenness* is wrong. What you consider *drunk* is between you and God. Sit with Him and ask Him about what He says you are permitted in this area. Obey Him and do not judge others based on what they do. Our bodies are His temple, they are not our own.

Weight: Well, I don't think there is any scripture that refers to ones ideal body weight, but man how this is a top priority in our world!! What we look like does not matter to God though– He only looks at our hearts! He created you, so He thinks you are perfect and beautiful however He made you. The Word *does*, however, refer to Gluttony as a sin— and oh how I commit this one!! Why do churches never discuss this one? Why is this one so permissible in our society, and even *encouraged* in the USA? Have you ever looked at the portion sizes in restaurants? It is ridiculous! But what's more ridiculous is that I can eat the entire thing, still get dessert and leave the place ill because I am so full! GROSS– and sinful! It really is, people.

Or, on the opposite end of the spectrum, a friend may exercise for 3 hours a day and focus hours of attention on what she eats, or fears eating and deprives herself of food. All of this is harmful to her *temple*.

Or, the quest for a perfect body being more important than the quest for a close relationship with Jesus. Idolatry is sin. The greatest commandment is to love God with all our heart, soul, mind and strength; to love others and to love ourselves! Not to worship our bodies, as many do, and call it physical fitness.

Worry: The Bible clearly refers to worry as *not trusting in God*. We are not supposed to worry. It doesn't add a day to our life. It sickens our bodies, our Temple of the Holy Spirit. How many of us go without rest because when we lay down to sleep our minds are consumed with worry, fears and doubts? We don't sit during the day because of all the crap that we need to be doing around the house or the office. We are harming our bodies when we do this. WE NEED REST!! God thought it was so important that He made it one of the *10 commandments*, people! As big as "Do not commit murder"!!!

When referring to the Sabbath, God is not saying to serve and work and then worship Him on that day! The Sunday Sabbath that we all think about– He is saying to REST!!! He made the earth, and then rested on day 7. Our bodies are designed to need 1 day out of 7 to rest. It is how He created you!! None of us do this. And THAT is a sin!!! It is a sin against God and against your body.

What does a day of rest look like to you? It will be different from mine I'm sure. On my Sabbath I do not put on makeup, I do not fix a meal, or wash clothes, or clean house, or do anything for my kids or husband that I don't *want* to do. I may go to the beach, read a book, take a nap, or I may spend time with a friend, have lunch, pray and listen to music. I usually don't get a *full* day, only a few hours, but I intentionally set this aside in my schedule once a week– or, at least, I *try* to. IT IS IMPORTANT. Our temples need this!! God cares about me so much that He *wants* me to Rest!! He *wants* to refresh me and strengthen me during that rest. We need to make this a priority!

Well, this some crazy writing today, but it's what God downloaded while I was in the shower. Take what speaks to you and disregard what doesn't. I pray that you search these issues out for yourself, with your Creator! He loves you and longs for you to come to Him and sit for a while!!

I love you, Karen

Tour de' Forgiveness

I never liked Lance Armstrong. When I first heard that he and his wife were divorcing, with 3 kids under the age of 5, I assumed he had cheated. I guess that was just my jaded opinion at the time, based on my own life experiences. I just assumed that was the reason— why else would they end it when everything seemed so perfect? All that being said, I was not a fan, I don't care how many bike races he won!

So, I never followed his career, never read any stories about him, never bought anything "Livestrong". In fact, I didn't even hear about all of the doping allegations or admittances surrounding him in these past few years, or any of the more recent news over the past few months. I was just *not* interested.

I did, however, watch his interview with Oprah– assuming that I would dislike him even more after it all. I was surprisingly mistaken. All I could feel was sorrow and intrigue, and Godly fear.

Mind you, as I was watching these interviews last week, I was not in a good place personally. I was harboring, and living out, lots of unforgiveness towards my hubby. It was a case of many many things piling up on top of each other. The dry-erase board in my mind was filled with lists of all the wrongs he had done and continued to do– and I had no intentions of using the eraser! They were staying there and I was rereading the lists over and over, and adding to it daily! Why erase it when I would have to rewrite it the next day?

Do you ever do that? IT'S NOT A GOOD PLACE TO BE. The Bible calls it *bitterness* and *keeping score. It* says:

Another dies in bitterness of soul, never having enjoyed anything good.
Job 21:25

Bitter roots grow up to cause trouble and defile many.
Hebrews 12:15

Each heart knows its own bitterness and no one else can share its joy.
Proverbs 14:10

Love…keeps no record of wrongs.
1 Corinthians 13:5

Yea, bitterness is *not* good. I was not experiencing a lot of "joy".

So, poor Lance Armstrong didn't stand a chance with me, or so I thought. But, as I watched the interview, my heart was stirred and stirred. I took notes on my phone. All I could feel was sorrow for him. I know you are probably saying "He is full of it. He had to confess, he was busted". And I agree with all of that. But, I was looking at the whole interview with spiritual eyes– and God was working something out in me during this time, all last week and up until today! Let me explain……

Lance starts out with confession. He answers "yes" to all of the big questions that Oprah asks; did he dope, did he lie, did he bully people? In this interview, after 10 years of saying "No", he finally admits that he has been lying and answers "Yes". I could see that he wanted to be free. He even quoted **John 8:32**, *"The truth will set you free".* Yes, He longs to be free, but this is only the beginning. You could tell he was saying and doing the right things now by confessing, but he still was not convinced in his heart. Because the beginning of **John 8:32** says, *"If you hold to my teaching, you are really my disciples. THEN YOU WILL KNOW THE TRUTH, and the truth will set you free."*

Jesus says, *"I am the way, THE TRUTH, and the life. No one comes to the Father except through me."* **John 14:6**

Lance Armstrong doesn't know "THE TRUTH"– yet. But, he will.

So, back to the interview. As I sat there watching him confess in front of millions of people, I wondered what that must be like. I mean, Catholics go into a box with just the priest, and I confess in my quiet time with just me and God. Maybe sometimes I confess to a friend, but not to EVERYONE THAT KNOWS ME. Can you imagine admitting to your greatest sins, your biggest mistakes, in that manner? I was wondering what God thought and the first word I heard was, "MERCY". I wondered, when the cameras stopped rolling, did Oprah offer Lance the love, mercy and grace that Jesus offers us? I wanted to tell him that so badly. Then I heard a little voice questioning me, "Do you offer that to those in your life when they wrong you?" I just ignored it— clearly God couldn't be talking to *me*. How could I want to show mercy and grace to Lance Armstrong whom I don't even like, and yet I withhold it from my own husband or kids? Man, I've got issues!!

Somewhere in the interview, either Oprah or Lance referred to "unforgivable sin". I think they were referring to him suing the people who had told the truth about him, and about him bullying them. Yes, the stories were horrible; the number of people that he had hurt and the lives he had affected by his dishonesty and bad behavior were many. But, NO SIN is unforgivable.

Psalm 103 says to, *"Praise the Lord, my soul and forget not ALL His benefits- who forgives ALL sins, and heals all your diseases, who redeems your life from the pit and crowns you with love and compassion, who satisfies your desires with good things so that your youth is renewed like the eagles"*.

Jesus said, *"People can be forgiven all their sins and every slander they utter."* **Mark 3:28**

So, what EXACTLY did Lance do, in God's eyes? Let's break it down. He cheated in a race and he had to lie more and more to cover up his cheating. The magnitude of his "sins" *seem* bigger to us because of his celebrity status; because of the arena in which he lived, because he makes so much money, and because he has worldwide corporations like Nike sponsoring him– whatever. To God, he is just like you and just like me. He cheated and he lied to cover up his cheating. It's no different than speeding and, when questioned by the cop, telling him that I didn't know it was 45 when actually I had just seen the sign and I was doing 70. I'd try to justify this by saying it was just a "little white lie", but it's NO DIFFERENT!!!!!

In fact, if you examine the details of Lance's "doping", you'll realize that it *did* start out small. He took a few cortisone shots early on; I mean, you can legally take that for swelling or some other condition, but he took it with the intention to help his performance. *That* is the definition of *cheating*. Then, just like any door that we open to the enemy, the sins get bigger and bigger. He ended up getting blood transfusions with dope in it. Man, that is a huge deal! But, I bet he had never thought that he would be doing something like that on the day that he did his first cortisone shot. The enemy deceives us with the *little* things and then turns them into *big* things right under our noses.

If you listen to his interview, Lance admits that he didn't think it was wrong when he was doing it. He justifies it by saying that he was, "leveling the playing field"; meaning, everyone was doping, so it was okay– Just like I'm sure, "everyone lies to the cops when they get pulled over", so it's okay, right? I don't think I had even thought much about how wrong that really is, until this very second. What other small lies, deceptions, stealing and cheating do we do in business, at work or at home, that we justify as just a little, small thing, or that *"everyone* does it"?

Switching gears– no pun intended– Lance goes on to talk about how he did what he did and got away with it for so long; the "loopholes", he called it "Scheduling". If he took the stuff on certain days and then got tested, he could test clean. Whatever– I say, "LOOPHOLES"!! As a Christian, I am constantly looking for loopholes to get around things that may be wrong, so I can justify doing them. But, "Just because something is technically legal doesn't mean that it's spiritually appropriate" **1 Corinthians 6:12 MSG**.

I am really blown away by the fact that cancer did not turn Lance to God, as most people do when faced with a 50% chance to live! They turn their life to God, or at least PRAY!

Nope, Lance said he was determined to do everything HE could to beat it, and he DID! He assumed it was his *own* strength that beat it. So, of course he believed he could win a Tour De France. I mean, he *had* just battled death and won, why not a bike race! Little did Lance know of why GOD had spared his life– and it's all playing out in this interview.

Further into Part 2 of the interview, Lance talks about his son standing up for him and Lance having to tell him the truth and telling him to, "Stop standing up for me". It is the only time in the interview that he begins to cry, to break— but he quickly gains his composure. Funny how, when things affect our children, they suddenly become real. He had been living a life of lies for over 10 years, yet he wept at the thought of his child lying for him. I wanted him to stay in that moment and just cry, but he's not there yet.

He went on to talk about his punishment. Of course, financially it was huge. Lance says he lost $75 Million in one day. He was asked to step down from the *Livestrong* Foundation, which *he* had started. He was banned from *all* forms of competitions; he can't even run in a 5k race. For someone who was made to compete, I could tell that this devastated him. A competitor is all that he had identified himself as. So, to tell him he couldn't compete anymore, in *anything*, I am sure he feels that he has no purpose. Reputation smeared, no credibility, no future race to prepare for— what is he going to do with himself? Oh, God has a plan for Lance Armstrong. *"'For I know the plans I have for you', declares the Lord"…"* **Jerimiah 29:11**

One profound fact that I heard in the interview, which was sort of overlooked even by Oprah, was his comment that his mom had always taught him to "never look back". He says that she never looked back or talked about the past. In fact, he had never asked even one question about his biological father, whom he does not know; and his mother has never said one word about him. THIS IS HUGE!!!!

This is the root. And that root grew and bore *much* fruit. He does not know his earthly father. He has been lied to for his entire life, regarding whose he is or how he was created. Yes, mom maybe never brought it up, but I can't imagine that, as a child, he never asked why he didn't have a father. Lies began— either by omission or actual false testimony. Do you see the vines of this thing growing up all through his life? The striving, the performing, the perfectionism to please a "father" that he doesn't even know exists. Trying to prove that he is worthy to be loved. From this point on, in the interview, I can't help but see him as a little boy sitting there.

He talked about his ex-wife, Kristin. Funny how he asked her if he should make a comeback, and only with her permission did he do it. She had one condition— that he *not cheat*; and he swears that he didn't. Why did he care what she thought? He said that she was very spiritual and that he didn't agree with everything she did, but in the end, he wanted her advice— he valued her opinion. Clearly, he felt God in her and he respected that. Interesting. Because, whether one walks in it or not, people know THE TRUTH when they experience it in other people. Do people experience THE TRUTH when they are with *me*? I don't know.

And the last thing Oprah had to say was a quote from **John 8:32**, *"The truth will set you free"*.

I believe, with all my heart, that Lance Armstrong will be set free and his life will be REDEEMED— once he fully humbles himself before God, asks for forgiveness and accepts Christ in his life. He may never receive forgiveness from the multitudes that he has hurt or betrayed, but forgiveness from God is a promise which leads to Redemption! All the earthly successes, fame and fortune he acquired in the name of Lance Armstrong will be miniscule in comparison to what can be done in the NAME OF JESUS!!

Lance may never know his earthly Father, but I pray he comes to know My Father, Our Father, the One and Only True God, who loves Him with an everlasting love, who forgives all His sins, and healed him from cancer and continues to heal his heart.

Today I awoke and read an article in our local paper about Lance entitled, "Armstrong's sorry, all right— sorry he got caught". It reminded me about my own unforgiveness. This writer is clearly still pissed at Armstrong and did not see what I saw in his interviews. Lance Armstrong deserves forgiveness; not because of who he is, but because of who Jesus is. It is a command from God for us to forgive, if we want to be forgiven. *"For if you forgive other people when they sin against you, your heavenly Father will also forgive you."* **Matthew 6:14**

So, I got out my eraser and cleared the dry erase board in my mind, and with God's help forgave my husband all of it; because God first forgave me and because no sin, or multitude of sins is unforgivable. I asked God to forgive me for keeping score and I asked Hayden to forgive me for the way I had treated him. I was set free immediately; joy and peace returned again.

I encourage you to forgive Lance Armstrong if you are pissed at him, and join me in praying for him. And, if you are like me, keeping a dry erase board in your mind, get out your eraser!! Do not allow any bitterness to take root and grow.

You too can be set free by forgiveness!

AMERICAN IDOLS

Well, the 11th season of *American Idol* is coming up in January, and I have watched it every year since the beginning with Kelly Clarkson. I love the show. I have come to realize that I love music and I love seeing people who have God-given talent using their gift, their voice. Anyway, this is not about the show, but about the fact that AMERICA, this nation I love and the only one I have ever called home, is full of IDOLS. I worship idols all the time— I am only now realizing this.

Do you even know what an idol is? I think of the idols in the Bible; little gold statues that people worshipped instead of the true God. Well, I don't have any of those around, but hold on a minute…

The dictionary defines an Idol as a representation or symbol of a deity or any other being or thing made or used as an object of worship; That on which the affections are strongly or even excessively set… hmmm

An object, or person, or thing that is greatly adored… hmmm getting warmer.

A Pretender, an imposter… interesting!

So, anything that I put *before* God is an *idol* in my life. My affections are strong towards my children, my husband, my friends— is *that* wrong? *If* it is stronger than my affections for my God, then YES!! That is Idol worship. And what does the Word say about Idol worship? Well, for starters, the first of the 10 Commandments commands us to have no other God besides God! It also says, *"Do not turn to idols or make metal gods for yourselves. I am the LORD your God."* **Leviticus 19:4**

I went on to read the Old Testament in Leviticus. Back then, God actually spoke out of the sky and through prophets. He warned them, He told them to tear down all of the altars built to other gods. I mean, I don't have any altars built to Buddha in my house, but oh I do have idols.

Remember, I said an idol is anything on which my affections are strong, anything I adore, anything I spend my time thinking about and worrying about. Anything I love with all my heart. Yes, my kids and my husband are an idol. I look to what I spend my days doing, my hours in a day. Most of the time is spent preparing my home for their return, cooking and cleaning for them, running errands. Believe it or not people, I don't sit around all day in my house reading magazines and watching TV, laid up on the couch. What my daily list consists of reveals to me where my priorities lie.

I have been assuming, up until this point, that this is GOOD!! Well, it *is* my job as a homemaker, and I do pretty good at that job when I am providing for their needs. Just like if you are working as an employee, if you are doing your job assignments and getting them done; then you are doing a good job. You are a success. Yes, you are a success in your boss's eyes, and I am a success in my family's eyes— but I wonder what God thinks of me. Well, that would take *time* with Him to actually listen, and right now I don't really have a lot of that! Don't you know it's Christmas time, and all the other crap that I gotta get done? Hmmmmmm... interesting.

My friend, Shara, had me listen to this song one day in her car. I immediately got chills and have listened to it probably 15 times since then, and every time I get chills. It's by Jimmy Needham. You will definitely want to listen after reading this.

Jimmy is a singer and musician, so he titled the song "Clear the Stage". But, if I were writing it, I probably would have titled it, "Clear the List", or "Clear my Mind", or "Clear the House", or "Just make some room *somewhere* for God to be able to speak to me". Sounds like a pretty good title, don't you think? LOL

"Clear the stage and set the sound and lights ablaze if that's the measure you must take to crush the idols. Jerk the pews and all the decorations too until the congregation's few and has revival!" [1]

What if I really took the time every day to spend with God; meaning, I put *everything* else on hold until I hear from Him, and get revived? *That* would be God worship. My idols would fall.

This writer is a singer, It's what he knows; and he is even attempting to worship God and feels like he is doing it with his singing, but he is still doing it wrong. I feel like I am living and doing my job as a homemaker, a wife and a mother, and I get shit done— but living is more than just *doing* and getting stuff done. What does God think of my day? Do I even care, or do I only care about what my little idols think?

Well, I do get offended when my idols don't like what I cooked. Or I get my feelings hurt when my idols don't even thank me for all my hard work. Sounds like I really care about *their* opinion— of course I do, I worship them, I idolize them. When this is the case, the opinions of those you idolize matter the most!!!

Imagine how different I would feel if I had visited with God and did what *He* needed me to do for the day. Then, when it was complete, and if the other people in my life were not happy with the results, their opinions wouldn't matter. What God says about me would stand above all other opinions!!

The good thing about that is, God sees us through the blood of Jesus. Meaning, He does not see our sins or our faults. He sees us as His perfect child, created in His image. Wow, he must think a lot of me!! I wish I saw myself as God sees me! Well, if I took more time to spend with Him, I would get more of that. Ya know how when you are with a really encouraging friend, who you know really loves you for who you are and you leave that conversation feeling so good! Why do I keep myself from God? Why do I prevent these awesome encounters by being too *busy* for them? I think part of me is just now realizing that I didn't even know what I was doing.

"Take a break from all the plans that YOU have made and sit at home alone and wait for God to whisper. Beg Him please to open up His mouth and speak and pray for real upon your knees until they blister." [1]

Ok seriously, who prays this long? KNEES BLISTERING??? But I get it. There are lots of times that I go to God, with all good intentions. I pray, I give him the list of things I need him to do for me. I confess and ask for forgiveness, lift up some prayers for a few people, then I'm off to do all the crap I gotta do. I mean he understands right? He knows I'm busy!

But, what if I just sat for a little while longer? What if after I got done *talking* and *asking*, I just *listened*? I've had many moments with God where I heard Him clearly. I have heard many words spoken to me at different times that changed my entire outlook on life; *"You are my beloved. I chose you Karen"*, when I was feeling fat and ugly and unloved— whoa, how that turned my day around! Or when I was worried about finances, how are we going to pay for all the crap we gotta pay for, and I hear Him whisper *"I got this"*, and I KNOW IN MY SOUL that He means it! LOL Makes me want to go shop!!

"Shine a light on every corner of my life until the pride, and lust and lies are in the open." [1]

How can I ask for forgiveness when I don't even realize some of the things I am doing? If we sit with God long enough and really ask Him to uncover things in us, He does; then we can ask forgiveness and it will be removed. I recently have been convicted about *selfish ambition* and *envy*. That sounds really bad I know, but it was in me, and operating in all kinds of underlying ways. I asked God to remove it. I couldn't do it on my own. I don't want to be envious or selfish! I really don't. I don't know what happened, but I feel different. My actions are different. IT IS WORKING.

"Read the Word and put to test the things you've heard until your heart and soul are stirred and rocked and broken." [1]

I know sometimes the Bible is hard to understand, with confusing and weird stories. But, when I really get quiet with God and read something, it comes alive and I understand. It pertains to my life and my daily situations. IT IS THE LIVING WORD OF GOD!! It is POWERFUL. It can be used as a weapon!! But only when it is professed out of your mouth *and* kept in your heart— *and* understood! When it gives you chills, when it stirs you, brings you to tears, when you *feel* it!! Sit with God and this happens.

"We must not worship something that is not even worth it! Clear the stage, make some space, for the ONE who deserves it!!!!" [1]

Please, go to itunes and download this song by Jimmy Needham: *Clear the Stage*. Sit for a while with God and let Him speak to you through it! I want to hear that you get chills too!!

1.   Jimmy Needham, *Clear the Stage*, Song Lyrics,
http://www.songlyrics.com/jimmy-needham/clear-the-stage-lyrics/

Having Issues with Church

I've got issues with church lately. I know God is trying to show me something. I have an aversion to anything having to do with *organized religion*. If I'm invited to a service, or concert, I have a hesitation. It's weird, because I used to live for this stuff!

And, I am noticing that I squirm anytime "money" is mentioned. When they take an offering, I get pissed. What is that? I do not have an issue with giving. I love giving to God's work. So, I talked with God about it this morning.

Have you seen the TV series, *The Bible*? If not, YOU MUST watch it! It completely brings the stories to life! It is anointed television! I am so excited to see God infiltrating Hollywood! Anyway, as I watched the scenes of the apostles' lives after Jesus ascended to heaven, I was convicted!! The early church looks nothing like what we call Church in 2013. Our churches are so far from what Jesus' mission to the apostles stated; "*Go and make disciples of all nations, baptizing them and teaching them all I have taught you.*"

We have gotten so caught up in programs, groups, making life cushy and fun for the Christians who come to that building called "church", that we have forgotten what Jesus *said* to be doing. We are so far from what the early apostles' lives looked like. They walked around with the POWER that raised Christ from the dead OPERATING in their lives!! They were healing people, Casting out demons, freeing people, breaking out of prisons!! Not running kid's programs and having meetings about how to raise money for buildings.

Nowhere in this BIBLE mini-series are the apostles talking about M-O-N-E-Y!! And nowhere in the written Bible either!! They are not concerned whether they will have enough food to get from one location to the next!! They just go and do. What do they have? FAITH!!!

Well, I say it is probably easy for them to believe— they just spent years IN THE PRESENCE of Jesus!!! Could you imagine getting to live with Him, walking around town with Him, having lunch with Him, listening to His stories, Him touching you and hugging you!! It was easier for them to believe. But even with all that, THEY STILL DOUBTED!! But, once the Holy Spirit came to live in them, there was no more doubt!! They believed, and they experienced Christ working through their own hands!!

They had FAITH!!! They didn't worry about provisions!! I feel our churches today worry first about finances, and everything they do is an attempt to draw people in so they can pay their bills. I KNOW their intentions are good and they are led by anointed leaders, but our churches are doing something wrong!!! And I feel it starts with the money thing!! Even without our knowing, the enemy has infiltrated American Christianity in a conniving way. We *think* we are serving God and ministering to people through these huge buildings, small groups and massive concerts, etc etc... but where is the POWER??? The apostles had no resources!!! All they had was their own eye-witness TESTIMONY and the POWER OF THE HOLY SPIRIT!!! That's it!!

It was all that was needed *then* and it is all that is needed *now*! I cannot bring one soul to Christ!! It is the Holy Spirit in ME that does the work!! I can be obedient and do what God says by interacting with the person etc., but only Christ, through me, can change a heart.

I'm reading a devotion by Rick Warren today, about Waiting on God. He quotes **Matthew 6:6** from the Message that says to find a quiet, secluded place so you won't be tempted to role play before God. WOW!! How often do we "Role Play"? I do it all the time. I find myself becoming a really good actress. Karen Hubbard, starring as "The good Christian." I get dressed up, looking my best, put my smile on, say Hi to everyone that I see, and enter the sanctuary. We are the cute little family, attending church on Sunday morning. Am I role playing or am I being *real* before God? Well, some days "being real" would look a whole lot different... barely rolling out of bed, looking like crap, feeling depressed and overwhelmed, in tears before God and everybody over the turmoil of my life. You ever have those days? But, then we fake it, put on a smile and our "costume", and head off to church. Well, who are we doing THAT for? The congregation? The pastor? I say to myself, "Well, I wouldn't want them to see how messed up I am", "I don't want anyone to feel sorry for me", "I am supposed to have more faith than this right", "I can't fall apart in the middle of church", "Hold it together, hold it together"— For *who*?

In CHURCH it is hard to be *real* before God!!! Now, on the back porch or in your quiet place, that is different!! So why are we, as Christians, spending so much time and money creating these "Temples", where it is difficult for all individuals to "get real with God" and even harder for non-believers to even think about entering the doors? Is *this* what Jesus was talking about when He gave the Great Commission? Is building up "country-clubesque temples" that cater to the members really reaching the lost who need to know the true Jesus?

I had an incident happen this weekend at the ball field, which is where I am for the majority of my current life. The coaches for the other team were acting like arrogant jerks— no other "Christian" way to say it. They were doing whatever to win, and running their mouths. When they won, and the game was over, they ushered both teams to the mound to pray. At first I liked the idea. We *should* come together to give thanks for God's protection during the game. But, one of our player's moms said that she was pulling her child because of how hypocritical that was. She said, "Those guys acted like jerks and now they are gonna go out there and *pray*, and act like they are 'good Christians'". She wanted her son to have no part in it. I disagreed at the time, because I was thankful that someone thought it was a good idea to give thanks.

As I contemplated this later, I was convicted. There were things I even regretted saying that day in the heat of the game. Like saying, "See ya!!!" to the 10 year old precious little boy in the cute uniform that my kid had just struck out! How awful is that? And I call myself a Christian!! If I would have gone to the mound to pray and confess to the public my belief in Jesus, I would look like a hypocrite too, to the nonbelievers. I don't know the intentions in the hearts of the coaches who led that prayer; were they doing it for show, were they humble and honest before God or were they trying to do the right thing, for the masses watching to think they were really good guys, good Christian men? I don't know. Was God honored by their show of adoration, or was He embarrassed? Only God knows those answers.

I was convicted. I am surrounded by unbelievers. I am in close relationships with lots of families who do not know Jesus and care nothing about going to or joining a church. They hate the idea of it— and now I am understanding why! As I listen to their reasons for not wanting to go to church, I see the enemies plan to keep them from God at work IN THE CHURCH. I hear, "All they want is our money", or "so and so goes there and acts all holy on Sunday and then is an unethical business man who doesn't pay me when I do a job", or "What's the point of going? I went to that church once and no one talked to me. I felt like an outsider. People are all trying to be the same, and its fake", "It's all a big show".

As true Christians, who want to bring the Kingdom to all people of the world, to bring the lost sheep to Jesus, shouldn't we care about what the lost think of us? JESUS CARES ABOUT THEM!!! HE WILL LEAVE ALL OF US SAVED ONES TO GO AFTER THAT ONE LOST SHEEP!!! He will leave us behind in our "safe temples" and go out in search of the lost ONE!! Shouldn't *we* be doing that? As a CHRIST FOLLOWER, shouldn't we get out there and FOLLOW HIM IN HIS SEARCH???

The lost are not coming to our temples!! Get out and *search* for them!! Interact with them, befriend them, and accept them where they are! Do not judge them from your "high place". I want to be in HIS PRESENCE, following HIS LEAD, HE is MY SHEPERD!! Most likely Jesus is not hanging out in the temple!

Who are the lost sheep that He is calling you to? It's not about leading them to the temple. It is about leading them to safe pasture, to quiet waters, *restoring their souls*! This can only come through meeting Jesus!!

Who will you be JESUS to TODAY??

The Great Power of Our Words

It is about to be the Thanksgiving Holiday and I am reminded of a real MIRACLE that God delivered last year during this time. I'll begin my story about a month or so before, when a friend of mine gave me a little book; 20 small pages that really changed my perspective on "words." It is called *How You Call It Is How It Will Be*, by Kenneth Copeland.

I know we have heard "words can kill", "sticks and stones may break my bones but words will never hurt me", "you better watch your mouth", "from the heart the mouths speaks", and so on and so on. But have you ever really sat and thought about what you are saying out loud? I know I tell my kids not to call each other names, not to say things like "I'm so dumb," knowing it hurts their self-esteem. But, until I read this book I had not thought about the POWER that is actually behind words.

Did you know that the world we live in was actually called into being by God, with words? —"Light be," and there was light. Copeland states that, this is a WORD ACTIVATED world we live in; it was created that way and it will always be that way. And, if we are Christians, professing Jesus as our Savior, we have the same power that Jesus has with words! THAT IS AMAZING!! AND IT'S TRUE!

So, think back to Jesus' time on earth. He saw blind people, he spoke and they could see; to the lame he said, "pick up your mat and walk"; in the storm on the boat, Jesus said, "Peace, Be still" and the sea was calm. His spoken word made things happen! Can you believe that we have the same power to speak things into being? Well, it's true. We can, *"Call things which be not as though they were"* **Romans 4:17**. The Word says *"Truly I tell you, if you have faith and do not doubt, not only can you do what was done to the fig tree, but also you can say to this mountain, 'Go throw yourself into the sea,' and it will be done. If you believe you will receive whatever you ask for in prayer"* **Matthew 21:21, 22.** Do you notice that it states, you have to SAY to the mountain to move? WOW, words have power!!

So, on with my story. After reading this book and being amazed by it and sharing it with friends, I began trying to watch my words. It was hard! It surprised me how much negativity came out of my mouth! It is hard to speak positively when the circumstances around you may not be positive! It's hard to believe! But I began to spend time journaling and writing down every worry, and then trying to find a scripture truth about that issue. The Word is full of real truth!! There is a scripture for EVERY incident on this earth!! Really, there is. Try it and see! Well, I was doing it; writing the scriptures out and trying to profess them daily, but not really seeing any change in my circumstances.

Here is the real reason that I'm writing. Over Thanksgiving we went to Atlanta to see Hayden's family. We were driving back Friday night and our dog Bo, who if you don't know him is like one of our children, began to get sick. We were about 90 miles outside of Auburn, so we knew we could take him to the emergency clinic there. He was very ill, acting really strange, and almost passed out. I knew in my soul that it was an emergency. We got to the hospital and sure enough he had a mass on his spleen that was bleeding. He had lost 25% of his blood volume and they said he would have died in the car if we had not stopped. They put him in ICU, gave him blood, and tried to get him stabilized for surgery. We began to pray.

Remember, it's Friday night, before the Alabama/Auburn game— and we're *in* Auburn. There were no hotel rooms, but God came through and miraculously got us one, through the help of my friend Amy. That's 6 people in 1 room, but we were thankful!

I was up all night praying! I was so afraid that he would not make it to surgery. We had been here before, with our other lab Sadie. It was just over a year ago when we had got a call in the night that she died. We had left that hospital $6000 in the hole, hearts broken and without her. It was a terrible time and I feared we were reliving it. Why would this time be any different? BUT I PRAYED and I BELIEVED! I spoke the truths of the Word OUT LOUD all night in that hotel room, as my family slept around me. I got on my knees next to the bed and professed that I KNEW GOD could heal him! Even a DOG!! He cares about EVERYTHING that we care about!! I was anxious and scared, and even doubted what I was saying, BUT I said it anyway! I could not sleep! Finally, just before dawn, I felt like I heard God say, "HE is going home with stitches". Ya know, how you can hear something and really believe it? A peace came over me and I was finally able to get to sleep.

Bo had surgery the next day to remove his spleen and a grapefruit size mass. The doctor's prognosis was not good. They immediately began to speak to us about chemo and treatment, and that his life expectancy, even with treatment, would only be about 9 months to a year. They used the words, "what we typically see in these cases..." it could be three things; a cancerous tumor, a benign tumor, or a hematoma (which is like a deep hard bruise). They said that 80% of these cases that are presented to the hospital, with a bleed, is cancer and it is very aggressive. As the young doctor spoke, I felt the urging from the Holy Spirit to stop him from *speaking*! He was professing words over my dog! He was speaking things that I did not agree with! He was CONVINCED, based on his past experiences, that BO had cancer!

I did stop him. I said something like, "well there is a chance that it could not be cancer, right?", and "we believe in prayer and are going to be praying for a miracle". He said he would pray too! He continued to give us the scenario of what we would go through when the test results came back. We would need to return in 10 days for the first round of chemo.

As I sit back now and remember this, I knew in that moment we would not be returning there. Well, it took about a week and Hayden got the phone call for the test results. The doctor was unsure and even waiting to tell us because the test results came back as a HEMATOMA— no cancer. The doctor said they were even going to take another sample, just to make sure. The doctors were surprised that they were wrong!

They had not factored in the power of prayer! They did not know that, as they were dissecting tissue and sending it to pathology, we had every believer that we know praying for our dog. It was the first time a dog had been prayed for by the prayer team with *Business Edge* in Destin. As people asked me about the situation, I told them that I believed it was *not* cancer. I spoke that out, instead of what all medical science said it would be. I knew the power of my words!

I am telling you all this to encourage you! Our God cares about every detail of YOUR life! He sees what you are going through and wants to help! He has given us the Word of God, The Bible, to speak His truth to EVERY circumstance! He has given you and me the power to profess things like we want them to be, and the power to change them!

I know some of you are realists, just telling it like it is. Well, that may be what it looks like in the natural, but we also live in a spiritual world! Start telling it like it is in the spiritual! If you are having financial worries, profess that "My God will provide all my needs according to His riches in Christ Jesus". If you are sick in some area, profess that, "By His stripes I am healed". Search the Word for yourself and find the truths that you need for whatever you are going through.

This has given me such a shot in the arm of HOPE!! We are so thankful that God healed Bo, but I am not finished. It encourages me so much to press on, to keep praying, keep speaking truths, to keep going, knowing that God sees me and cares about the little details of my life! He cares about you too!

It has been almost 1 year since Bo recovered in that hospital. He did not have another visit to Auburn Veterinary Hospital, as the experts had predicted! He is strong, happy and healthy, and we thank God every day for allowing us more time with him.

BELIEVE THE WORD!! SAY IT OUT LOUD!!

YOUR WORDS CAN CHANGE THINGS!!

GIVING

A few days before Thanksgiving my kids and I gave of our time and volunteered at the Harvest House, handing out Thanksgiving baskets. It was so much fun— it feels so good helping people. But, that was not the real blessing on this day....

I saw a young mom, about my age, with 2 daughters on that day. I only saw them briefly, and we never spoke, but the image stuck with me. I wanted to know their story— I just felt a connection to them.

Well, my busy, crazy, life goes on. We traveled to Atlanta for Thanksgiving with Hayden's family. I began my ridiculous amounts of shopping and returning, and shopping again, seeking out the best presents for each of my kids, while at the same time trying to keep it even and fair. They are all rotten, and yes I overdo it every year; it's one of my many issues! I was extremely stressed out and overloaded on responsibilities, most of which I am certain God did not ask me to do.

There was one thing that He *did* require of me— to bless another family this Christmas season. So, I prayed for God to show me who to bless. And every time that I prayed, I saw the face of that blond-haired child we had seen in the Harvest House. I didn't know how I would find her, but I was CERTAIN that God would lead the way. I did not doubt that one bit. So, I called the Harvest House director, Lori, to asked if she remembered this family; single mom, blond, attractive, two beautiful girls the same age as my kids. Lori said that she had seen hundreds of families in the last few weeks and had no recollection of this family. I *still* did not doubt. I called Lori the next day with a few more details, to see if I could come look at the list of people she had served. It was just too many, but she would look again. She called me back, leaving a message, saying that she thinks she has found my family. So, as I was giving some donations to the Harvest house the next day, I stopped in her office. She was excited to tell me about the family; a mom who had recently had cancer, three teenage girls, "that's your family right?" I said, "No, that is not them". Lori explained the situation of this family, which was dire, asking me if I could help them. Their situation was upsetting, the mom was really really sick. But I insisted that God was SPECIFIC about the family I was to help, and she agreed with me that God would have me meet them somehow. I left there a bit discouraged, but I said to God in the parking lot, "I guess you will have me run into them somewhere!" Again, I did *not* doubt.

That evening, it was a chance occurrence that all 4 kids were home at the same time. I asked them if they remembered the family from Harvest House, and I described what I remembered of them. That is when Avery pipes in, looking over her phone, when I didn't even think she was listening and says, "Yea, I saw that girl in the hall today at school." I said, "Really? Do you think you could point her out in the yearbook?" And within 5 minutes we knew her name, "Hailey". So, I called Lori and she located them. She called Davina, the mom, and this is where our encounter began!

I met with Davina and her girls in Barnes and Noble, and immediately felt a connection. She is a beautiful girl. She is 34 but looks 22, really! You could tell she was a good mother, just trying hard to provide for her family any way that she knew how. She is selfless, hardworking and so humble. She did not accept my help easily, and she even urged me to help a less fortunate family than hers. As we spoke further, she wanted to help *me*! I found that she has published a coloring book online and knows the ins and outs of publishing for FREE! I was so excited! God has told me that I am going to write a book and I knew this meeting was also part of that plan.

I could see how attentive Davina was to her girls, love just oozed out of them! In everything she said you could *feel* creativity! I began to see, so clearly, the plan that God had for her life, and all the

83

gifts and talents He had blessed her with. I could also see how the enemy had spoken to her through bad relationships, disappointments, broken marriages, hardship, and stolen her dreams and creative spirit. I was so excited for what God was about to do!!

So, the shopping began! It *is* one of my favorite things to do! I had a budget on what I would spend, but like any budget I try to go by, I ignored it. The money did not matter! In fact, as new ideas came for what to get them, I wanted to return presents for my own kids in order to buy more for this family, but I didn't. I just shopped and shopped as God lead me through the stores. The amount did not matter, as I knew I was doing the work of God Himself. All my money is His anyway. Avery and Piper helped. I cannot express to you enough about HOW SPECIFIC GOD IS!! If you really go through a store asking God to lead you to things, HE DOES!!!! You should try it if you never have— it will blow your mind.

We got clothes for the girls at Old Navy and Abercrombie. Cute outfits just like I would for my own girls. Avery and Piper picked out things in colors the girls would love. New Nikes, new furry boots, books I knew they would like. I bought a camera for Davina and an easel. I do not know a lick about art, and was actually in a hurry shopping at Michaels— and there were like 25 easels to choose from! I picked the one that God lead me to. I actually thought the wooden one would be better, but I listened to God and got the other one.

I was having a hard time with bedding for the girl's room, not finding anything I liked in numerous stores. While I was shopping in Marshalls, I spoke to Amy O'Keefe and she offered to give them the bedding set that she had from her girl's rooms, which they no longer used. In that instant, while still on the phone with her, I found throws and pillows to accent it in Hailey and Melina's favorite colors. In a matter of 5 minutes, the bedding was done! Things that we are not using do not belong to us. Thank you Amy for doing your part!

We wrapped each gift beautifully. Avery stayed up two nights past 12 to wrap presents with me. Oh how the thought of that blesses me! In fact, even the boys took time to wrap a gift.

So, on our last day of school, I checked the kids out early and we prepared to deliver the gifts. I met Davina at her kids' bus stop. She was waiting for the girls and couldn't leave yet, so we got her house key and went to their apartment. It was so neat and clean, and decorated so cute for Christmas. We left warm cookies, that my girls had just baked and decorated, on the counter and filled the area surrounding the tree with presents. It was a beautiful site! And we left. As much as I wanted to witness their reaction to the blessing, I did not want any "thank you". I wanted God to get all the glory and I wanted to leave room for the Holy Spirit to do a work through our giving. There were bigger blessings I wanted for each girl's heart that only God could give.

I am BLOWN AWAY at how God works. I am humbled to be asked to participate in HIS BLESSINGS. I am honored to serve such a good, loving God. I am encouraged that MY PRAYERS ARE BEING ANSWERED EVEN AS I TYPE THIS!

❖ *"A Gift opens the way for the giver, and ushers him into the presence of the Great."* **Proverbs 18:16**

❖ *"Excel in the grace of giving"* **2 Corinthians 8:7**

❖ *"He who gives to the poor lacks nothing."* **Proverbs 28:27**

❖ *" You will be made rich in every way so that you can be generous on every occasion and through your generosity will result in thanksgiving to God"* **2 Corinthians 9:7**

❖ *"If it is contributing to the needs of others let him give generously"* **Romans 12:8**

❖ *"It is more blessed to give than to receive"* Jesus, **Acts 20:35**

- ❖ *"The righteous give without sparing"* **Proverbs 21:26**

- ❖ *"Freely you have received, freely give"* **Matthew 10:8**

- ❖ *"Give and it will be given to you, a good measure, pressed down, shaken together, running over will be poured into your lap. For with the measure you use, it will be measured to you."* **Luke 6:38**

Please read the following letter from Davina to me. All I can do is weep. So get some tissues!

From: Davina
Subject: Our deepest gratitude
Date: December 27, 2012, 5:20 PM
To: Karen Hubbard

Just a few weeks ago I had imagined such a different Christmas. Money has been so incredibly tight this year, and most of my family was planning on being out of town for the holidays without any plans to do something here, and we had not even one Christmas decoration to our name. I was picturing a Christmas alone with my daughters, with no family gathered around, no Christmas tree, no decorations and only the two small gifts that I had bought by pinching money out of our rent envelope. I had been quite depressed over the whole thing, thinking how every year I had always given my kids a decent Christmas— at least with a Christmas tree. I was so sure that this year would be a sad disappointment for them. I was really just losing the Christmas spirit fast, thinking of how it would be so different this year and thinking how the girls would be so disappointed. (continued…)

I kept praying for the strength to not give up and get depressed, and for the wisdom to know what to do to make Christmas special with what little we had. I finally stopped worrying and let it go, just having faith that things would go as they were meant to. And if this year was different and not so great, then it was for a reason and something to learn from. It wasn't long after that things began to just miraculously fall into place, one after another. A lady that I clean house for had randomly asked me in conversation if I was getting our Christmas tree soon. I told her that we usually have a fake tree but that we had lost all of our decorations in the move last year and were just planning on decorating the tree in our yard. I told her how it was right close to our sliding glass doors, so it would be like it was in the living room. I was going to do lights on it and just make the most of that. I was actually pretty excited with our little compromise that the girls and I had come up with for the tree lol But then, the lady, Mrs. Theresa, had quietly packed up a box full of decorations for us and gave it to me when I had finished work. I was so surprised and so excited just thinking of the girls and knowing how happy they would be to decorate the house. I couldn't wait for them to get home that day to see the box of decorations. Then, the next day a friend of Mrs. Theresa's came by with *more* decorations! And THEN my dad came by with a tree! We were SO excited, our house actually looked like Christmas now. That's when I came up with the idea to pull everyone together for an early Christmas dinner. Now that the house looked Christmassy I wanted to share it and I really wanted to bring everyone together before they all left town for the holidays. My gift to everyone this year was going to be simply bringing everyone together and cooking some special things for them. Originally I had been stressed, thinking that in order to pull the dinner off I would again have to dip into the rent money. Even though we were doing this with everyone bringing a dish, I still had to cook at least two things. I figured I would just keep it cheap and we'd manage somehow. I really was just so happy to be able to give the kids a proper Christmas with decorations and the family around. The fact that I only had the small present for each did bother me, but

I pushed that thought aside in my mind and just remembered, that isn't what the holiday is about, and that's what I told my girls— they said they understood and were just happy to be together. The day that I was going to take money out of the rent envelope for the holiday food, I was on my way home from work and was planning on stopping by the house to grab the money and go get the stuff— Lorie called me right before I did. She started asking about what foods we needed for Christmas dinner. I was surprised and I was SO relieved, thinking I wouldn't have to take that money out, since I already had taken some out for their gift. Then she told me about you, Karen. That's when we talked and met. I really was just beyond surprised about the whole thing honestly. I had never had *anything* like this happen to me before. At first I was not sure what to do. I felt like, I knew we weren't doing so great this Christmas, but I didn't want to be selfish and take away from anyone else who needed this more than us. But, when you explained to me *how* you had decided on us and how you had found us, I got goose bumps just thinking that my prayers had *really* been heard. I still get goose bumps and it brings tears to my eyes thinking about it as I write. The way that you explained things, I realized that it wasn't about giving to the poorest of the poor, it wasn't about giving THINGS— it was about giving hope, love, compassion, blessing a family that was down on their luck and just needing to know that they were cared for and not forgotten. I realized that, more than anything, it was about god reaching out through you to me— not with just the physical gifts, but with the message that *hey I'm here for you and looking out for you guys and that, with faith, everything will always go as it should.* Things don't always go as we plan, but they do go as they should— and always for a reason. When I realized this and accepted the blessing, I still never imagined how amazing it would be. I think the girls, just like me, being guarded, we didn't get our hopes up for anything. I think life has thrown a lot of curve balls our way and disappointments, and so I just naturally tend to expect nothing more than what I have in hand. It's just the way I have learned to live— can't be disappointed if you don't expect anything. So, after we talked, I was hopeful that we would talk again and I could help you with your book. But, in truth, I half expected that I might not hear from you again— it all really just seemed too good to be true. When you met me at the bus stop that day I was pretty surprised. And then, when I went home with the girls afterwards I was picturing a few gifts under the tree, but when we walked in the door— Oh my goodness! We all stopped dead in our tracks with jaws dropped. Little Melina said, "What in the world!? That is the most presents I have EVER seen in my life!!!" They were just in awe and so was I. I couldn't believe it!

So, now we had Christmas decorations, family coming for Christmas dinner and a tree *full* of presents! It really really felt like Christmas! Then to make things even better, the girl's dad made a surprise decision to come down to see them. He brought their grandma, whom they hadn't seen in about 6 years— they hadn't spent a Christmas with their dad in years either. So, the girls had yet another surprise. It really was just one blessing after another this year. So amazing. And then, when we opened the gifts, I just could not believe it! I am still amazed at the things you got for us and how perfect it all was. Clothes that the girls needed so badly but that I couldn't afford to get them and shoes! The girls actually had holes in their old shoes and we were honestly just trying to make them last until income tax time, hoping for a good enough return that we could replace them, among other things we needed to take care of. And then the easel and camera! Wow! I am still in awe of those two gifts, so completely excited to have them. I don't even know how to begin to thank you for those two things. I tell you that my heart is over flowing with gratitude to you and your family and to god for blessing us with such a perfect Christmas— for giving the girls their hearts desires and for giving me mine as well. I feel like a kid with new toys lol I honestly have wanted a field easel for years but could never afford one. I had actually been planning to maybe have enough with income tax to either get the cheapest one they had or buy the materials and make one, so that I could get motivated to get back into my painting. And the camera! Just the few pictures that I have already taken with it has sparked my imagination and fueled my creative spirit. I feel so inspired and motivated creatively to create so many new things!

I know this letter is long and overfilled with my gratitude, but I feel like I can't express to you enough how very thankful we are for everything that you and your family have done for us. For the gifts, for your kindness and just for being the instrument of god that you have been in making our Christmas so special. The physical gifts that you gave us are so wonderful and amazing, we appreciate each one so very much, but even more so we appreciate the gift of compassion that you gave to us. I appreciate that my children, even if it's only once in their lifetime, got to witness a beautiful act of random kindness and an answered prayer. Thank you so much from the bottom of my heart for everything!

Davina and family

About The Author

Karen Hubbard was born the baby girl of six older brothers to Pete-a-Boy and Patsy Kuluz.

This began shaping and developing the mindset of being a princess at a very young age.

Karen's mission is for women to know they are loved, cherished and adored by The God that created them. Her passion is to discover and dispel the lies that women believe and live life in Abundance through the grace and Truth of Jesus Christ.

Karen and her husband, Hayden have been married for 5 years and combined have 4 children.

Karen never takes for granted that she lives in paradise, the Emerald Coast of Florida.

Made in the USA
Charleston, SC
16 December 2014